THE CENTERS OF CIVILIZATION SERIES

(Complete list on page 171)

GAZA

In the Early Sixth Century

Gaza

IN THE
EARLY
SIXTH
CENTURY

By Glanville Downey

NORMAN : UNIVERSITY OF OKLAHOMA PRESS

BOOKS BY GLANVILLE DOWNEY

Procopius, *Buildings of Justinian*
(editor, with Henry B. Dewing)
Loeb Classical Library. Cambridge, 1940.

Chronicle of John Malalas. Books 8–18
(translated from the Church Slavonic, with Matthew Spinka).
Chicago, 1940.

Belisarius, Young General of Byzantium.
New York, 1960.

Constantinople in the Age of Justinian.
Norman, 1960.

*A History of Antioch in Syria
from Seleucus to the Arab Conquest*.
Princeton, 1961.

Antioch in the Age of Theodosius the Great.
Norman, 1962.

Aristotle, Dean of Early Science.
New York, 1962.

Ancient Antioch.
Princeton, 1963.

Gaza in the Early Sixth Century.
Norman, 1963.

Library of Congress Catalog Card Number: 63–11020

K. G. D.   E. K. D.

in memoriam

Preface

"MAN MAKES HIMSELF in and through history, and that is why each generation only fully understands itself when it sees itself as a link in the chain of humanity on the march." These words of the distinguished French scholar Henri de Lubac reflect one important part of the task of The Centers of Civilization Series, namely to help the present generation to understand the past from which it has sprung, and thus to see the present in better perspective. This knowledge should help us, too, as we look forward into the future.

Though it made its own characteristic contribution to the preservation and transmission of classical culture, Gaza has been one of the less well-known cities of the late classical world, and the present volume is only the third book on Gaza published in English, the earlier studies being M. A. Meyer's *History of the City of Gaza* (1907) and G. F. Hill's translation of Mark the Deacon's *Life of Porphyry, Bishop of Gaza* (1913).

The present study is the first attempt in any language to bring together in the form of a book what we know about Gaza during the reigns of Anastasius (A.D. 491–518) and Justin I (A.D. 518–527) and during the early part of the reign of Justinian (A.D. 527–565). This period has been chosen for a volume in this series because it represents the flowering of the School of Gaza, the remarkable circle of literary men whose work played an important part in the development of Greek Christian literature and made Gaza one of the most prominent centers for advanced literary training in its day.

As a study in the history of culture, the present book takes its place alongside two other volumes I have been privileged to contribute to The Centers of Civilization Series, *Constantinople in the Age of Justinian* (1960) and *Antioch in the Age of Theodosius the Great* (1962). If read consecutively, in the order Antioch–Gaza–Constantinople, the three volumes together will illustrate three of the significant stages in the interaction of Christianity and the classical tradition in the developing Christian Roman Empire, in three cities which were different from one another and at the same time had a common basis. The volumes were, however, planned and written separately, so that each represents an independent study which can be read by itself. A fourth volume, on Caesarea in Palestine in the age of Eusebius, is planned. Chronologically, this will precede the volume on Antioch.

In keeping with the plan of The Centers of Civilization Series, this volume has been written directly from the ancient sources. It represents the results of study of Gaza and allied subjects over a number of years. My interest in Gaza originated with the discovery of a certain mosaic in the excavations of Antioch in 1933. As a result, I was invited to contribute a paper on the School of Gaza to the 1955 Dumbarton Oaks symposium on Palestine in the Byzantine period, and it is a pleasure to recall here my indebtedness to the symposiarch, Dr. Carl H. Kraeling, for the invitation. This paper formed the basis for an article, published in the *Harvard Library Bulletin* in 1958, which is the forerunner of the present book.

The extent of my debt to the work of other scholars will be apparent from the books listed in the Selected Bibliography. In addition I must acknowledge the assistance I received from Lionel Casson's delightful book *The Ancient Mariners: Seafarers and Sea Fighters of the Mediterranean in Ancient Times* (New York, Macmillan, 1959).

In quoting from ancient texts I have sometimes made my own versions, sometimes I have ventured to borrow from existing translations. The quotations from Plato in Chapter V are taken from Archdeacon Adam Fox's excellent book *Plato and the Christians* by kind permission of the Student Christian Movement Press, Ltd., London, except that the passage from the *Republic* at the head of the chapter is borrowed, with grateful acknowledgment, from F. M. Cornford's translation (New York, Oxford University Press, 1945). The passage from Photius in Chapter VII is borrowed, with thanks, from J. H. Freese's translation of Photius' *Library*, published in London in 1920 by the Society for Promoting Christian Knowledge. The translation from Pappus of Alexandria in Chapter VIII is based on the version published in my article in *Isis* in 1948. In the same chapter the passages from Choricius of Gaza are for the most part based on the version I supplied in E. Baldwin Smith's *The Dome* (Princeton University Press, 1950), though for the present purpose they have been condensed and in part paraphrased. The passages from the Liturgy of St. John Chrysostom in Chapter IX are reproduced, with the kind permission of the publisher, from the edition in Greek and English published by the Faith Press, Ltd., London (*The Divine Liturgy of St. John Chrysostom*, 3rd ed., n.d.). The description by Pausanias in the same chapter is based on the translation of W. H. S. Jones in the Loeb Classical Library, with certain adaptations of my own. The version of St. Paul's speech in Athens in the same chapter is quoted by permission from the New English Bible, New Testament, copyright by the Delegates of the Oxford University Press and the Syndics of the Cambridge University Press, 1961. The versions of the chorus in Sophocles' *Antigone* in Chapter V and of Cleanthes' *Hymn to Zeus* in Chapter IX are my own, both being somewhat abridged.

Once again I am indebted to Professor William M.

Calder III, who has given generously of his time to read the manuscript and has suggested many important improvements in it. Likewise I must record my thanks to Professor Irfan Kawar for procuring a topographical map of Gaza and its vicinity which I would not otherwise have been able to obtain.

G. D.

Dumbarton Oaks,
Washington, D. C.
April, 1963

Contents

GAZA

In the Early Sixth Century

Prologue: The Lives of a City

*Because it is the culmination of associations
existing by nature, every city exists by nature.*
— Aristotle, *Politics*

As he journeyed to his home after the end of the
Trojan War, the sagacious Odysseus "saw the cities of
many men and learned their mind." The opening words
of the *Odyssey* were no mere literary ornament; for like
any intelligent Greek, Odysseus took note of everything
that he saw, wherever he had to go. And even in those
early days of the Greek world, it was in their cities that
one could best come to know men and learn of their ways.

In the Graeco-Roman world, the Trojan War was
not far removed from the beginnings of history; and
throughout all of that history, the men of the "civilized
world"—that is, the lands of Greek and Roman culture
—had been traveling. Herodotus, "the father of history," had been able to write only after he had traveled
"to see the world," and if a man hoped to gain the best

3

education the world could offer him, he set out to see at least the major cities of his world.

This was far from being mere curiosity or restlessness. In the world of those days, the city was literally and completely the center of civilization. Man, as the master thinker Aristotle had written at the opening of his treatise on *Politics*, was "by nature an animal meant to live in a city." It was indeed, the master went on to say, man's nature that impelled him to live in a city. In the culture of the classical world, it was only in the city as a community of his fellows that man could reach his highest development, politically, socially, intellectually, spiritually. A collection of farmers, shepherds or fishermen, living and working in isolation, could hardly be thought of as developing the intelligence and the virtues of the dwellers in cities, who could, by conversation, inquiry, and disputation, learn from one another and enlarge their minds. Athens was by no means the only ancient city in which people were eager to spend their time either in telling or hearing some new thing.

And as in the Athens of St. Paul's day, it was not only the men of Athens itself who were thus curious. They were joined in their eagerness by "the strangers which were sojourning there." These strangers had come to Athens in their travels; for if the city was the focus of man's civilized life, every city was different from every other. Each had its own special history, its traditions, its pride in its own special achievement. It was in their own cities, as much as in their nation, that people felt patriotic pride. A cultivated man of those days was one who had been educated in the culture of a city. But his culture could not be complete unless he traveled to see and study the other great cities of his world—both the cities, that is, and their people. For the real end and goal of study was man himself. An educated man had to be able to understand himself and to try to understand his fellows, and it was by observing them in their lives in the civilized community that one came to understand men. Men shaped the community, and the community shaped men. Communities could not be learned about from books. One had to visit them and live in them.

So it was with the city of Gaza on the southern coast of Palestine in the early years of the sixth century after Christ. As classical culture spread beyond the original lands of the Greeks and the Romans, it came to cities with older histories and older cultures. Hebraic, Egyptian, Mesopotamian, Punic, Celtic roots—all could be found beneath the cities of the great Roman Empire. If it was one of the virtues of the Empire that it was able to hold together people of such diverse origins, it was one of the virtues of the Graeco-Roman culture that it was able to spread and make itself the dominant factor in communities of such different histories. And when Christianity came into this world, it found its path prepared by the earlier diffusion and acceptance of the classical culture and the classical tongues.

Thus it was not unusual for the Gaza of the Later Roman Empire, the cultivated and elegant Greek Christian city, to be a place of ancient Philistine origin. There were other Graeco-Roman cities of that day which had

5

biblical or prebiblical histories, such as Tyre, Sidon, and Damascus. Even Jerusalem had become in a certain sense a Graeco-Roman city, though its Judaeo-Christian religious significance remained paramount. What set Gaza apart from the others was its unusual history in having developed into a prominent Christian center of intellectual activity and literary culture when it had formerly been known both as a stronghold of the Philistines and a home of pagan worship. Most of the great cities of that day, such as Athens, Rome, Antioch, Alexandria, went back to classical origins, but Gaza was the only such city that could add its biblical history. The story of Samson as told in the Book of Judges not only formed a part of a religious tradition, but had a life of its own, in the form of the tale of the exploits of a romantic figure which in a world of heroes and demigods had its own heroic stature. The city of Gaza thus could claim an early history which other great cities, even the imperial capital, Constantinople, could not match.

By reason of its location, Gaza had always had a necessary part to play in the history of that region of the Mediterranean world. The city was in fact an essential link in communications, both north-south and east-west. On the ancient road that ran along the Palestinian coast, skirting the higher ground inland, Gaza was the last city before one set out on the desert road to Egypt, or the first Palestinian city that one would reach on the journey northward from Egypt. At the same time it was the western terminus of the caravan route that led from Petra through Beersheba, and its excellent harbor kept

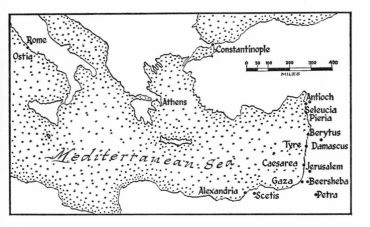

THE MEDITERRANEAN WORLD
OF THE EARLY SIXTH CENTURY

the city in easy and regular communication with the other Mediterranean seaports.

On the edge of the desert, Gaza played an essential role locally as the market center to which the wandering folk of the desert might come to obtain the products of the sedentary craftsmen of the town.

And so the history of Gaza was tied up with the histories of all the powers that had ruled that part of southern Palestine. The city had opened its gates to the Pharaoh Thutmose III, "the Napoleon of ancient Egypt" (*ca.* 1502–1448 B.C.), when he set out on the conquests which carried him through Syria and east of the Euphrates. As one of the five great towns of the Philistines (the others being Ashkelon, Ashdod, Ekron, and Gath), Gaza came under the control of the Israelites relatively late in its history. When Alexander the Great in his conquering advance marched south along the coastal road, Gaza was able to resist him for five months (332 B.C.).

Then, like the other cities of the strategic coast, Gaza suffered and changed hands more than once during the wars of Alexander's successors, the Hellenistic kings. Alexander Jannaeus, the king of the Jews, captured Gaza (96 B.C.), after besieging it for a year, and razed it to the ground. But there had to be a city in this place, and when it was rebuilt, some years later, Gaza embarked on a new stage in its history.

This was, indeed, a new era for the whole of the eastern Mediterranean, namely the beginning of the rule of the Romans which brought peace and a new prosperity in the expanding economic system of the Roman world.

When in 64 B.C. the Romans found themselves obliged to occupy Syria and Palestine in order to put an end to the anarchy into which the last weak Hellenistic kingdoms were falling, the new rulers of this ancient land were intelligent and practical in the political arrangements they made for the local peoples and their cities. Aulus Gabinius, who became proconsular governor of Syria in 57 B.C., started the actual rebuilding of Gaza, though the plan for its re-establishment must have been made some years previously.

From this time on, Gaza became one of the prosperous seaports of the Roman commercial empire. Shipping to the western Mediterranean the goods brought from the East by the caravans, as well as Palestinian wine, which found a ready market outside the province, Gaza found its place in the new Roman world and enjoyed all the benefits of the Pax Romana, which was built up on the basis of the Roman genius for law and order and the Roman understanding of the fundamental importance of good communications and the protection of travel and commerce.

Gaza shared in all the prosperity of the Empire, which meant that the emperors took care to see that the important cities, including Gaza, were cultured as well as commercially prosperous. Temples and public libraries were erected at imperial expense and the endowment of libraries and public professorships of literature and philosophy was a regular part of the emperors' activities.

Hadrian (A.D. 117–138), the "Olympian" emperor, who did so much for the cities of the eastern lands of his empire, visited Gaza several times, and, as grateful cities were accustomed to do in such circumstances, the people of Gaza established in his honor a public festival which was celebrated annually.

Relatively remote from the Persian frontier, Gaza had not suffered directly from all the vicissitudes of the Empire's history during the third century, when the increasing power of both the Persians and the barbarians put a strain on the Empire's defenses, likewise on its economic structure. The effort and the drain of resources came near to bringing about the real collapse of the Roman state.

But the Empire was saved by the military genius and statesmanship of a series of able emperors—Aurelian (A.D. 270–275), Diocletian (A.D. 284–305), and Constantine the Great (A.D. 306–337)—and with the first quarter of the fourth century a new era began for the Roman world, bringing to Gaza and the other cities changes which would affect their whole future.

These changes touched every aspect of life. In material affairs, the far-reaching reforms of Diocletian and Constantine put the army and the government bureaucracy on a new footing, which meant that the structure of the state became much more stable. But in order to support the enlarged army and the expanded bureaucracy, it was necessary—according to the economic and political thought of that era—to transform the Empire into a corporative state in which economic and social life and industrial production were under the direct control of the government. In order to assure an adequate supply of goods, workers were "frozen" in their occupations. Tradesmen were compulsorily organized in government-controlled guilds. The manufacture of weapons and military supplies remained a government monopoly.

All this transformation was in keeping with the development in the ideology of the imperial office. In order to enhance the prestige and power of the sovereign, the Roman emperor now became an autocrat exercising absolute power, and the imperial court was reorganized along military lines.

These were indeed radical changes, but they were deemed necessary to save the state in its outward aspect. At the same time there began a spiritual and intellectual transformation which was no less epoch making. In many ways, the chief event of the fourth century was the conversion of Constantine the Great to Christianity. From this there stemmed consequences which were to exert a great effect not only on the history of the Empire but on the whole future of the Western World.

In the intellectual life of the Empire, one of the results of Constantine's conversion was the emergence of the question of the relationship of Christianity and the old classical culture. In the early history of the Church, Christian teachers had been preoccupied with the typical aspects of pagan morality which so clearly ran counter to the doctrine of the Gospels, and from this point of view it seemed axiomatic to Christian thinkers that their faith and the pagan literary culture could have nothing to do with one another. The African lawyer Tertullian, having experienced a conversion to Christianity of massive proportions, summed up this point of view with his famous rhetorical question "What has Athens to do with Jerusalem? What has the Academy to do with the Church? What have heretics to do with Christians?"

This was a formidable question indeed, for the classical educational tradition, shaped about the study of the great works of classical literature, was at the basis not only of education but of public life and social intercourse. If there was to be a new Christian Roman Empire, must it cut itself off entirely from the ancient and traditional literary heritage of the old Roman Empire out of which the new Christian state had to be built? This was to be one of the questions of the century, and the solution of the problem, in the form of the harmonious absorption of the classical tradition into the new Christian culture, was to form one of the strongest bases of the new Christian world. Of the form which this culture reached in Gaza in the early years of the sixth century we shall see more in a later chapter.

A somewhat more specialized development of the new era in religion was the search for the sacred sites connected with the life of Christ and the transformation of Palestine into the Holy Land. Both Constantine the Great and his pious mother, St. Helena, were eager to discover the holy places and make them goals of pilgrimage. Constantine himself gave lavish grants from government funds for the construction of churches. Not only in Jerusalem, where the Holy Sepulcher, Golgotha, the Garden of Gethsemane, and other spots drew crowds of the faithful, but everywhere in Palestine shrines were built at the sacred sites, and from being one of the poorer and more remote provinces of the Empire, Palestine began to emerge as the chief earthly focus of Christendom.

Thus in the fourth century there began a process of transformation which in the eastern lands of the Empire was to find its culmination in the working out of a new Christian Greek culture which in time provided for the Christian Roman Empire (destined to become the Byzantine Empire) the source of its strength.

In this process every city passed through its own characteristic experience. Indeed, the process could hardly have been a uniform one, for every city had its own distinctive history and it was in terms of this history that the new culture had to be worked out. One of the influential developments took place at Antioch in Syria, as has been told in another volume of this series. Gaza had its own history, culminating in a spectacular episode which made it famous throughout the Christian world.

I.

Marnas and Christ

. . . until I make thine enemies thy footstool.
—PSALM CX

IN THE EIGHTH YEAR of the reign in Constantinople of
the most Christian Emperor Arcadius (A.D. 402), the
saintly Porphyry had been bishop of Gaza for seven
years. He was fifty-five years of age, and the seven years
of his episcopate had been a continuous battle against
the forces of paganism in the city and in the villages
around it. The struggle sometimes seemed almost dis-
couraging. Porphyry believed and trusted his Lord; but
even so he could not have foreseen when he went to Gaza
as bishop that he was to be the instrument of the final
suppression of the idols in the city.

It was nearly three generations since the conversion of
the great Emperor Constantine. The Empire had become
a new Christian Roman Empire, and the splendid new
capital, Constantinople, "Constantine's City," was one

of the great Christian cities of the world, filled with magnificent churches built by the Emperor. The other great cities in the eastern part of the Empire, Antioch and Alexandria, were centers of Christian learning. Jerusalem, the city of Christ's death and resurrection, was the goal of Christian pilgrims from all over the world. Throughout the Holy Land there were oratories, churches, and monasteries built at the spots associated with the life and labors of the Savior. Caesarea, the civil capital of Palestine and seat of the metropolitan bishop, had been a center of Christian scholarship for two centuries, its great library adorned by the names of Origen and Eusebius. The Emperor Theodosius (Arcadius' father) had issued a series of decrees designed to put a stop to pagan worship and magic rites. The hierarchy of the Church occupied a place of honor in public life alongside the officials of the civil administration, and Christian worship had become an established part of the ceremonial life of the imperial court.

But if the world seemed securely Christian, there were still in many places pagans, followers of the old religion, who had not yet been converted to the True Faith. These were arrogant folk, either superciliously standing aloof from the religion of Christ or fanatical enemies of it. It was proving by no means easy to turn the whole world to Christ. Christians were themselves secure in their faith, but they had constantly to be on their guard against the idol worshipers—just as they had constantly to try to bring them to the truth. Repeatedly the government had issued laws putting an end to pagan worship and ordering the closing of the temples. But the laws, if they were enforced in the beginning, soon fell into neglect, for many of the high officials everywhere in the Empire were still pagans and on occasion they could be bribed by the worshipers of the old gods.

It had fallen to Bishop Porphyry's lot to serve his Lord in no easy task. In some parts of the Empire, local conditions had brought it about that the pagan way of life had been able to survive in a whole community and even flourish. Heliopolis, also known by its Semitic name Baalbek, the city of the great god Baal, was one such place. Athens and Hierapolis in Syria were centers of paganism, and even in Antioch itself there were still numbers of pagans.

So it was that Porphyry found himself bishop of what was still predominantly a pagan city. This seemed remarkable for one of the principal cities of Palestine. Yet Gaza was not one of the holy places and it had never become in actuality a part of the Holy Land. In the early days of Bishop Porphyry's episcopate there had been just 280 Christians in Gaza, in a population of several thousands, and while the number had grown, the majority of the people of wealth and position in the city continued to be pagans. This had of course been true since the beginnings of Christianity; it was usually the well-dressed and educated, the wealthy and the wellborn who were the last to come into the Church, and it was these, the leaders of the city, who formed the core of the pagan tradition in Gaza. This was one of the many difficulties that faced a bishop and his clergy in a city such as Gaza.

It was only by the saintly example and the devoted labors of the Bishop, and by the faithful lives of his flock, that Christianity could be kept alive in Gaza at all. There was one Christian church, named the Church of Eirene ("Peace"), and a small house for the Bishop. In contrast, the pagans possessed eight fine temples. These were the shrines that one would expect to find in any center of paganism: the Temple of the Sun, the Temple of Aphrodite, the Temple of Apollo, the Temple of Athene, the Temple of Hecate, the temple of the Tyche ("Good Fortune") of the city, and a heroon, dedicated to a mythological hero, a shrine so ancient that the name of the hero had been forgotten.

The cult of Aphrodite in Gaza was typical of the heathen worship. In one of the public squares there was a prominent marble statue of the goddess, its elegant nudity a constant offense to the Christians. The pagans of the city, especially the women, lit lamps and burned incense before the image, for the goddess was supposed to give advice, in the form of dreams, to persons contemplating marriage. (The Christians pointed out that some of the marriages so contracted were unsuccessful.)

The greatest of the temples, however, was the Marneion, dedicated to Marnas, the powerful deity who was supposed to represent the Cretan-born Zeus. This was the most prominent pagan shrine in Gaza, a center where all the worshipers of the old gods came together. Marnas was the all-powerful deity who presided over all aspects of nature; he had to be propitiated if the city was to remain prosperous. The other gods and goddesses each presided over a particular sphere of human affairs, but it was Marnas who was supreme.

It was against such ancient powers that Bishop Porphyry and his people had to contend. The power of Christ would eventually be victorious, they knew, but the way ahead of them was hard. The pagans used every device to put down the Christians. Porphyry remembered his arrival at Gaza after he had been consecrated as bishop in Caesarea. The pagans who dwelt in the villages outside the city, when they knew he was en route, strewed the road with thorns and prickly vines and covered it with filth; and when the bishop and his party came into sight, the idolaters set by the roadside fires of evil-smelling substances, so that the travelers were choked by the stench and blinded by the smoke.

Such was the manner of life to which Bishop Porphyry found he had been sent. Yet his vocation carried him through troubles such as a young man of his origin might not have expected to face. Born of a noble and wealthy family in Thessalonica, the urge to forsake all and follow Christ had come to him in his mid-twenties. He had then left his home and had gone to Egypt, where he spent five years of solitary contemplation and prayer at Scetis in the Nitrian Desert, west of the mouths of the Nile. Egypt was full of ascetics who had gone there to rid themselves of attachment to the world and to master the desires of the flesh.

After five years of this ascetic training, Porphyry

18

made his way to the region of the Jordan, where he spent another five years of prayer and adoration, dwelling in a cave.

One of the rigors which the ascetic of those days imposed upon himself was a diet of the most meager kind. This was thought to be one of the sovereign means for the mastering of the body and its desires. As often happened, Porphyry began to suffer from an ailment of the liver, with recurrent fever, the diet being such that the liver could not function properly. But Porphyry despised the disease, and from this time on, for the rest of his life, he followed a regimen which kept the body in a continual state of mortification and set him free for the service of God. On ordinary days he never ate before sunset, and then his meal consisted of stale bread and herbs. On the holy days of the Church, however, he ate at noon, and on these days he added to his diet oil, cheese, and peas and beans soaked in water. He would also take, for its medicinal effect, one cup of wine mixed with water.

When he had finished his five years in the cave near the Jordan, Porphyry went to Jerusalem to worship at the holy places. Here, by his saintly life and deep piety, he attracted the notice of Praylius, the bishop of Jerusalem, who ordained him to the priesthood and appointed him custodian of the wood of the True Cross, kept in a golden coffer. Porphyry was forty-five years old.

It was such a man that was chosen, three years after his ordination, to be bishop of the notoriously pagan city of Gaza. It was a post that called for the greatest courage and constancy and the most burning love of Christ.

For several years after his arrival in Gaza, Porphyry devoted himself to his flock, all the while observing the pagans and coming to know what their strength was. He lived in the little bishop's house with the greatest simplicity, attended by two young men who had devoted themselves to his service. One of these was a calligrapher, a professional penman named Mark, who had been making his living copying books in Jerusalem when Porphyry was there. Attracted by Porphyry's saintly life and his winning courtesy, Mark attached himself to the Bishop and eventually wrote his biography. The other companion was a lad named Barochas (Baruch), a waif whom Porphyry had come upon, sick and abandoned, in the street in Gaza. The Bishop had taken the child into his house and restored him to health, and Barochas had become his faithful attendant. Both Mark and Barochas were in time ordained as deacons by the Bishop.

From his experiences it became plain to Porphyry that he could not hope for the assistance of the local authorities in the enforcement of the imperial laws according to which the pagan temples ought to have been closed. The pagans at Gaza were too strong, and they were able to pay out bribes which kept their rites safe from interference, legal or otherwise.

So Bishop Porphyry, three years after he had come to Gaza, sent Mark to Constantinople with a letter to the patriarch, John Chrysostom. The patriarch secured the issuance of an imperial order that the temples of Gaza should be closed, and a commissioner was sent from Constantinople to put the decree into effect. The commissioner, Hilarius, did indeed close all the temples except one. But that was the shrine of Marnas, and Marnas' devotees conveyed to Hilarius a bribe of such proportions that he abstained from closing the shrine. Hilarius left Gaza, and it was not long before the idol worshipers had resumed their accustomed rites.

This episode made it plain to the Bishop that he himself would have to make an appeal in Constantinople and that it would have to be made in the highest quarters. Taking Mark with him, he set out on the long voyage to the capital and spent many months there at court. He found a number of other bishops in the capital on similar errands.

Porphyry was soon able to win the attention of the Empress Eudoxia, a pious lady then expecting her fourth child, who was to be the future Emperor Theodosius the Younger. Eudoxia, hearing the Bishop's story, went to Arcadius and asked him to order that the pagan temples in Gaza be destroyed. The Emperor's reply showed what difficulties attended the suppression of the old religion. Arcadius knew that the city was primarily pagan, but he also had to bear in mind that the city paid a considerable sum in taxes, and moreover paid regularly, something that was not to be expected of every city. If the pagans, who were the majority of the population, were suddenly deprived of their worship, they would leave Gaza and settle elsewhere, and the revenue would be lost. The Emperor proposed instead to proceed gradually, taking away civil dignities from the leading pagans and ordering the temples to be closed rather than destroyed.

The Empress, however, less bound by mundane considerations, assured Bishop Porphyry of all the help she could give, and furthermore—something the Bishop had not requested—Eudoxia promised the funds for the foundation of a new church in Gaza. In time, all that Porphyry could wish for was granted. When Theodosius was born, shortly afterwards, a son following three daughters, the Emperor was persuaded, with some difficulty, to grant the petition for the demolition of the temples; and as the Bishop left for Gaza, Eudoxia gave him a considerable sum of money for the new church, as well as a fine set of liturgical vessels, plus funds for the construction of a guesthouse connected with the church. The carrying out of the imperial orders was entrusted to a commissioner, Cynegius, who was an active Christian.

The Bishop set out for Gaza thankfully, but he knew that there would still be a battle, for the pagans would not accept the imperial orders without difficulty. Ten days after he reached the city, in company with John, the metropolitan bishop of Caesarea, Cynegius arrived to put the imperial decree into effect. The commissioner was accompanied by a number of civil officers and a large body of troops. It was the middle of May, A.D. 402.

The imperial officials found many of the pagans gone from the city, for when they had learned of the Emperor's action, the idol worshipers perceived that this time they might not be able to resist. Many of them, including the majority of the wealthy men in the city, left

Gaza. Some planned to stay temporarily in the villages near the city, while others went farther and settled in other cities.

Cynegius quartered his soldiers in the houses left empty by the departed pagans and next day summoned a meeting of the people of the city, at which he read the imperial letter. The citizens learned that the temples and their idols were to be burned.

Uproar broke out as the pagans shouted in protest and the Christians cried out for joy. Cynegius ordered the troops to move into the crowd, and the soldiers began to beat the pagans with clubs and staves.

Now began the scene which was famous in the history of Gaza. Mark described it in vivid detail in his biography of Bishop Porphyry.

At command, the troops moved out of the square to begin the demolition of the temples, and the crowd of Christians eagerly followed. This was no unusual assignment for the troops. Roman soldiers were employed in peacetime for many nonmilitary tasks, notably engineering operations, and they were amply familiar with the techniques of demolition. Just one hundred years previously the Emperor Diocletian's troops had opened the last great persecution of Christianity by tearing down the Christian church in Nicomedia.

Because it was the principal pagan shrine of the city, the soldiers went first to the Marneion. Here, however, they could accomplish nothing, for the priests of the god, having had warning, had reinforced the gates of the inner temple with great stones, so that it was impossible for the soldiers to break them down. The priests had also, as was discovered later, hidden the idols and the precious vessels used in the rites.

It was decided to deal with the Marneion later, and the soldiers marched toward the other temples. This time they had no trouble in making an entrance. They first seized whatever valuable objects the temples contained, then demolished some of the shrines and burned others. The work was orderly, for Bishop Porphyry, speaking at a service in his church, had laid a curse upon any Christian citizen who should take anything for himself from the pagan temples. The Bishop himself, with his clergy, stayed with his people during the demolitions and restrained them whenever temptation became too much for them. There was, however, some looting by strangers who happened to be in Gaza at the time and had joined the crowd.

Ten days were spent in tearing down and burning the temples and destroying the statues. Finally, the Marneion alone remained standing. There were various views as to what should be done with it. Some said that it should be demolished, others that it should be burned. Still others thought that the temple should be ceremonially purified and converted into a church, as had been done in other cases.

Seeing the disagreement, the Bishop proclaimed a day of fasting and prayer, so that the Lord might reveal to the people what His will was. In the evening, Porphyry celebrated Holy Communion, and during the service a child seven years old, speaking in Aramaic, cried out that the temple was to be burned. Having questioned the child and his mother, the Bishop was satisfied that no one had taught the boy to say what he did, and the child's message was taken to represent the will of God.

Next morning, the soldiers and the Christians of the city gathered and set out for the temple. The preparations for burning the building were carefully made. The stout wooden doors of the inner sanctuary were smeared with a mixture of liquid pitch and bacon fat. The combination was highly combustible and the whole temple was soon in flames. The soldiers and the strangers, when they could get inside the building, looted what they could of the ritual vessels and other valuables. The fire burned for several days.

After this, the troops and the Christian citizens went around to all the houses in Gaza searching for idols. They found many in the courtyards of the houses, and these they either burned or threw into cesspools.

This was all that the Bishop and his clergy could have hoped for. But the destruction of the temples and the idols was only the beginning of new labors, for many of the pagans now begged to be received into the Church, and there was the question which was usual on such occasions, namely whether such converts could be considered sincere. The Bishop declined to make distinctions, however, and received all who wished to be converted. It was recorded that in that year about three hundred people in Gaza became Christians, and every year thereafter the number increased.

It was an old tradition that a church should be built

on the site of a demolished pagan temple as a perpetual symbol of the triumph of Christianity. There was now debate about the plan and style of the church that was to replace the Marneion. The temple itself had been a handsome structure—a domed, circular building surrounded by two porticoes, one within the other. A circular plan for a church would have been quite acceptable, but the Empress Eudoxia, who was providing the money for the construction of the church, wished it to be cruciform, and sent a plan from Constantinople.

The site was cleared of ashes and of the remains of the marble work—much of the marble had been reduced to lime by the fire—and, again following a well-established tradition, Bishop Porphyry had the remnants of the marble laid as paving in the street outside the temple. For ritual reasons, women had not been allowed to enter the Marneion; now not only women, but dogs, pigs, and beasts of burden would walk on its fragments. This desecration grieved some of the idolaters even more than the destruction of the temple itself, and for many years thereafter such citizens of Gaza as continued to be pagans would not walk on this part of the street.

Bishop Porphyry engaged the services of an architect named Rufinus who came from Antioch and so was well acquainted with the best styles of architecture. When the time came to begin the work of construction, the Bishop proclaimed a day of fasting, and when he dismissed the people after Matins, he bade them gather at the site of the new church next morning, each bringing a mattock or a shovel or other such tool.

26

In the early morning the people met at the Church of Eirene, to go in procession to the site of the Marneion. It was a traditional procession, beloved of the Christians of those days. First came Barochas, bearing the Cross. Then came the Christian folk of the city, escorted on either side by a file of the soldiers whom Cynegius had left in the city to deal with any counterattack by the pagans. At the rear walked the Bishop, bearing the book of the Gospels and surrounded by his clergy—like Christ with His disciples, as people said.

As they marched, the people sang—in Greek—the opening verses of the Ninety-fifth Psalm:

O Come, let us sing unto the Lord; let us heartily rejoice in the strength of our salvation.

Let us come before his presence with thanksgiving; and show ourselves glad in him with psalms.

For the Lord is a great God; and a great King above all gods.

In his hand are all the corners of the earth; and the strength of the hills is his also.

The sea is his, and he made it; and his hands prepared the dry land.

O come, let us worship and fall down, and kneel before the Lord our Maker.

For he is the Lord our God; and we are the people of his pasture, and the sheep of his hand.

Other psalms followed, and at length the procession came to the site of the Marneion. In the traditional ceremony of the foundation of a building, the architect

Rufinus took gypsum and marked out on the ground the plan of the edifice. While the people knelt, the Bishop prayed and then bade the digging of the foundations to begin. Crying out "Christ hath conquered!" all the people began to dig. There was no difference between men and women, or old men and children, but everyone worked with all his strength. Some dug up the soil, while others carried it away, so that in a few days the trenches for all the foundations were ready.

The stones were now prepared in a quarry outside the city, and the Bishop again assembled the people at the site. After prayers and much singing of psalms, the Bishop himself began to carry stones and lay them in the foundations. He was followed by all the clergy and the laity. The people sang as they worked, and the singing could be heard three miles from the city.

The work went ahead rapidly, and when the time came, the Empress Eudoxia, according to her promise, sent thirty-two columns of the famous emerald-tinted marble ("Cipollino") of the promontory Carystus in Euboea. When these columns reached the harbor of Gaza after their sea voyage, the whole population, men, women, children, and old men, ran to the shore. Each column was laid on a wagon and the people themselves pulled the heavy burden to the church.

The building of the church, carried out by hand, went forward carefully and slowly, for the builders knew that the stones had to settle. The work lasted for five years. The church, when completed, was called the Eudoxiana in honor of the Empress. Along with its great burdens, the imperial office also carried the power to give great gifts, and generosity was one of the qualities expected in an emperor and his consort. It was indeed from its public buildings, churches, and endowments that the imperial house derived a considerable part of its prestige.

The great ceremony of consecration took place on Easter Sunday, April 14, A.D. 407. The service was the most magnificent that Bishop Porphyry could prepare. There were present not only all the Christians of Gaza and the neighborhood but many of the bishops of Palestine and a large number of distinguished laymen from many cities. There were in addition a thousand monks. There was feasting and rejoicing throughout the week following Easter Sunday.

People came to visit the church from great distances. Bishop Porphyry was sometimes criticized because he had made the church so large when there were still relatively few Christians in Gaza. He replied that people must not have little faith and that he himself was of good hope that Christ would multiply his flock and that in time the congregation would grow so much that the church would have to be enlarged.

This was Bishop Porphyry's monument, and it marked an epoch in the history of the city of Gaza.

Porphyry was bishop for fifteen years more. One final episode in his life is recorded by his biographer, Mark the Deacon, a characteristic picture of life in the Christian community of Gaza—and indeed in the Christian world as a whole—in those days.

Even after the destruction of the Marneion and the

clear manifestation of the will of the government, paganism was not dead in Gaza, and the Christians, clergy and laity alike, had to be ready at all times to deal with unbelievers. Christians and pagans had constantly to encounter one another in all the ordinary business of life, and as natural enemies they not infrequently found that their business transactions turned into matters of contention.

A personal quarrel thus begun could grow into a major incident, and this was what happened on one occasion when a dispute arose between the steward of the Eudoxiana and one of the officials of the city administration who was a pagan. An argument over the payment of taxes on some land belonging to the church became noisy enough to attract some of the other city officials, and then some Christians joined in. The idolaters were still in the majority in the city, and on such an occasion they did not hesitate to produce clubs and even swords, although the manufacture of weapons was supposed to be a government monopoly and it was illegal for civilians to possess arms.

The private recriminations grew into a riot, and seven Christians were killed and many others wounded. The rioters set out in the direction of the Bishop's house. Fortunately, some Christians were able to run ahead and give the Bishop warning. Bishop Porphyry judged, rightly, that this was not an occasion on which he ought to offer himself as a martyr, and with his companion, Mark the Deacon, he made his way to the flat roof of the house and hurried away, crossing from one roof to the next.

When they arrived, the pagans broke down the doors of the Bishop's residence and, disappointed in not finding him, proceeded to wreck the house. Meanwhile, Porphyry and Mark, as they fled across the roofs, met, on one of the roofs, a girl about fourteen years old who recognized the Bishop. When the girl greeted him, he found that she was an orphan, working to support an invalid grandmother. She was not a Christian but had long desired to become one. It was on the roof of this girl's house that the Bishop and his companion found refuge. The girl promised not to reveal their presence and supplied the Bishop with a straw mat and a pillow made of chaff on which he might sleep.

The girl offered her guests the very meager food which was all she could afford; but this was in fact not unlike the Bishop's accustomed diet. He and Mark stayed overnight on the roof until they knew that the rioting had ceased. Returning to his home, the Bishop found Barochas lying there, severely wounded by the rioters. The governor of Palestine sent troops to Gaza and the rioters were punished. But paganism still was not dead in Gaza.

In time Bishop Porphyry died, on February 26, A.D. 420. He had been bishop of Gaza for twenty-four years, eleven months, and eight days. He was seventy-three years old—a ripe old age in the world of those days. If Gaza was not yet wholly Christian, the religion of Christ was firmly established in the city. The Bishop, by his

31

life and his labors, had become a part of the tradition of the city. In all his works, he had been a part of the community, a member of the community as well as its leader. The Christians of Gaza, together with their chief pastor, had shown one of the reasons why Christianity was replacing paganism: Christianity was the religion of the individual as a part of his community, the earthly community in which he was a part of the Body of Christ, while paganism was the religion of the independent individual seeking to find his own salvation by his own efforts in a mysterious and often hostile world in which the pagan as a solitary creature had to work out his religion for himself. It was in the manner in which the Marneion was destroyed and the Eudoxiana built that one could see the strength of the Christian community as a community; and it was thus that an ancient pagan city was being transformed, in due time, into a new Christian city. Physically, of course, it was substantially the same city; it was the people who were being changed. Bishop Porphyry's name lived in the history of Gaza as a symbol of the coming of the new city.

II.

The Faces of a City

*A city comes into existence because no individual
is self-sufficing; we all have many needs.*
—PLATO, *Republic*

THE MEDITERRANEAN WORLD always faced on the sea
—*mare nostrum,* "our sea," in Julius Caesar's phrase—
and much of the life and prosperity of the Roman Empire depended upon its seaports.

These seaports naturally had many things in common.
But they were also ports on the coasts of Egypt, Palestine, Syria, Anatolia, Greece, Italy, Gaul, Spain, and
Africa, and thus they naturally also differed one from
another. The merchant, the traveler, the soldier, the government official—all came to recognize the differences
and the characteristics which distinguished the many
harbors of the Graeco-Roman world.

Arriving at Gaza, a traveler would at first see many
things that were familiar to him. A busy port such as
that of Gaza was filled with ships of all kinds, from row-

33

boats and tiny fishing vessels to heavy merchantmen and the trim warships of the imperial navy. The rowboats and fishing boats, when not at work, were drawn up on the beach or tied at the stone quays. The larger vessels sometimes lay beside the quays, especially when loading or unloading; sometimes they rode at anchor in the harbor. At times one could see them moving slowly about the harbor, warped by oar-driven skiffs.

The fishing boats were of a design that had been used in the Mediterranean for centuries, broadly and solidly constructed, their lapstreaked hulls brightly painted. The single mast supported one sail, sometimes a square rig, sometimes a fore-and-aft or lateen sail. But the boat could also be worked with oars, and there was a large oar at the stern for steering. When the boats were drawn up on the beach, sails and nets would be spread out to dry in the bright sun, and the fishermen, having disposed of their catch, would be busy washing and mending the heavy nets. Many boats represented a family enterprise, and one could see a grandfather, sons, and grandsons all at work together. Sometimes they spoke Greek; more often their tongue was the indigenous Semitic speech of Palestine. The water front itself was a babel in which one heard Greek, Latin, and Aramaic, plus the Egyptian speech of visiting sailors and merchants.

Among the bigger ships, Gaza almost always had in its harbor one of the large merchantmen which carried the busy trade of the Mediterranean world. These were of all sizes, from the great liners of twelve hundred tons down to the smaller vessels which made their way along the coast, calling at every port and picking up cargo and passengers for short trips.

The largest cargo and passenger vessels sailed between the major ports, sometimes carrying several hundred passengers in addition to cargoes of wheat, olive oil, wine, or lumber. Some of the larger merchantmen were able to carry twenty thousand gallons of the fine wine of Palestine, which was exported all over the world. The wine was transported in earthenware jars which were carefully sealed and stowed upright. Sometimes a ship of the great grain fleet carrying wheat from Egypt to Constantinople would put in at Gaza, but whenever possible, these vessels preferred to make the trip nonstop. This fleet was vital for the well-being of the capital, whose population was so large that the surrounding area was unable to furnish sufficient food. The capital required more than one hundred thousand tons of grain a year, part of it for free distribution to the poor and the unemployed.

The merchant ships were built on a pattern that had been developed by centuries of practical experience. Built with rounded hulls, they were often designed to use sail and oars together. Stem and stern posts curved in graceful lines, the stern rising high out of the water. Both for the sake of cargo space and for safety, most ships were wide in beam. A typical merchant ship was 184 feet long, 45 feet in the beam, with a hold 44 feet deep. This could carry between 1,200 and 1,300 tons of grain. There was a cabin on the after part of the deck for the captain and officers; the crew and passengers slept on deck, not a hardship in the warm Mediterranean climate, in which the sailing season, to escape the winter storms, lasted only from April to November.

The main element in the rigging was always the square mainsail carried on the single mast in the center of the ship. The larger vessels carried a triangular topsail above it, the apex of the triangle attached to the top of the mast. Forward, there was usually a bowsprit sail carried on a short raking mast projecting over the bow. Some ships, in place of the square mainsail, carried the fore-and-aft rig or something resembling the lateen sail of later centuries. The canvas sails were brightly colored, and with their gay paint and gilded ornaments the ships in harbor made a fine sight in the clear Mediterranean air with the bright sun reflected on the blue water.

Some merchantmen were equipped only with sails but others used oars in addition. Usually the oars were arranged in a single bank running the length of the ship, unlike warships, which carried two or more banks. The rowers were slaves or prisoners, though sometimes they were free sailors.

The ships were steered by a pair of large oars, linked together, which projected along either side of the stern. The captain had to navigate by the sun and stars and to use landmarks wherever he could, for there was as yet no compass. Many ships preferred always to travel within sight of land, though the larger vessels on long runs would take to the open sea. There were maps and coastal charts which were fairly accurate, and there was a handbook of harbors which gave practical information.

Ship's crews could be got together in almost any port, and the best of them were highly skilled. The Greeks had been building ships and sailing for centuries. They loved the sea and had an instinct for it, and were in some ways as much at home on water as on land. Egyptians also made capable sailors.

If he could have looked at these ships, a sailor of later times would have said that they carried less sail than they were able to and that the masts were much lower than they need have been. The result, of course, was that the ships were slow, but they were that much the safer. In good weather, with a following breeze, they were capable of making between four and six knots, but in poor weather a captain would be content with two. Merchants and travelers alike were prepared to be patient. Readers of the Book of Acts knew that St. Paul's famous voyage from Caesarea (up the coast from Gaza) to Rome had lasted from August to March—although, to be sure, that included three months spent on Malta following the shipwreck, further sailing being impossible in the winter months. But it was never possible to keep to a schedule, for every voyage was entirely at the mercy of the weather. If winds were not favorable, the voyage from Gaza to Constantinople, a distance of about one thousand nautical miles, required twenty days, including stops en route. The passage from Alexandria to Ostia, the seaport of Rome, took anywhere from fifty to seventy-five days, depending on the weather.

The glory of the Mediterranean waters, however, was the splendid warships of the imperial navy. The Mediterranean headquarters of the fleet was at Seleucia Pieria, farther north along the coast, but warships were a not unfamiliar sight in the harbor of Gaza, where they sometimes put in during their training cruises or fleet maneuvers. The navy was still essential for good order on the seas, for in spite of all vigilance there were still outbreaks of piracy from time to time; and fast vessels were frequently needed to carry imperial emissaries on their official errands. Besides, the Vandals, who had conquered North Africa, had a powerful fleet in the western Mediterranean and while they showed no signs of trying to expand eastward, the navy had to be on guard at all times.

On the basis of long experience, the imperial admirals had brought to the highest development the best types of fighting ships. The great triremes, quadriremes, and quinqueremes of former days, with their multiple banks of oars, had been gradually given up in favor of smaller and lighter vessels. The two classes now most used were the Liburnian galley and the new type popularly known as the *dromon,* or racer. Both of these were often seen in the harbor of Gaza.

The Liburnian had an amusing history, having originally been invented by the pirates of the Dalmatian coast, who needed fast ships which would maneuver quickly. This galley had so many advantages that the Roman fleet soon adopted it. The pirate version had had a single bank of oars, but the Romans added a second bank, giving a total of fifty oars on each side of the ship. The ports and oarlocks in the two banks were not placed directly above one another but were staggered, and the oars were of different lengths, so that the two banks did not interfere with each other. One of the advantages of the model was that it was possible to lower the mast and rigging to the desk while the vessel was under way, thus making it possible for the ship to go into action with no delay. As with all ancient warships, one of the principal features of the Liburnian's armament was the ram, a massive timber, sheathed with bronze, which projected underwater from the bow.

The ship's complement consisted of oarsmen, marines, archers, and artillerymen equipped with heavy catapults which could hurl stones with accuracy, even at sea. The oarsmen were free enlisted sailors, more dependable, and capable of being better trained, than slaves. In a fight, success hinged largely on the captain's being able to maneuver the ship with split-second precision, and the rowers had to be both strong and willing to react instantly to the boatswain's orders. The sailors and oarsmen were principally Greeks from the Ionian coast of Asia Minor and Egyptians.

But the new marvel of the imperial fleet was the *dromon,* a kind of destroyer which was able to attain great speed and was invaluable for scouting and communications. This was a single-banked ship provided with a deck which protected the oarsmen. An important innovation was that the crews of these vessels were trained both as oarsmen and fighting men, so that there were no superfluous men on board, and in an action every man would count.

Such were the handsome ships that could sometimes be seen riding at anchor in the harbor of Gaza. Painted blue and white, the colors of the imperial navy, with gilded ornaments and bright signal flags and lanterns, they made a fine sight.

As the visitor walked along the quays or the beach in the hot sun, all the varied merchandise of a busy seaport would be spread out, waiting to be loaded. The caravans which had come overland, via Beersheba, from the East had brought spices, rugs, silk and cotton goods, and packages of precious stones and choice metal work. From Iran, India, and East Africa came furs and hides, embroideries, perfumes, and drugs. Because of the cost and the risk of transportation, all these caravan goods commanded high prices, but there still was a greater demand for them than could be supplied.

The spices added their pungent contribution to the varied smells of a water front, all adding up to the typical harbor smell compounded of pitch, hemp, spices, salt air, charcoal from kitchens and ovens, and human functions. The quays were filled with a babel of noises coming from men and their animals, for donkeys and camels were an essential part of any such scene. Beside their burdens, recently unloaded, lay or stood the camels which alone could transport such goods across the desert. Their haughty expressions and supercilious airs would seem comical if one did not know what extremely difficult creatures they could be.

It was not only the exotic goods of the Oriental caravans that made the water front of Gaza a fascinating spectacle. The products of Palestine itself which passed through the seaport were many of them famous and in demand all over the Graeco-Roman world. Staples among the exports were wine, dried figs, and dates. Fruit and date plantations were highly profitable and the products were much in demand. Date syrup made in Jericho was popular; the wine produced in Galilee was famous. Various kinds of fruit wine were also made and shipped overseas. Whole villages were kept busy making the earthenware jars (the "shipping containers") in which the wine was transported.

Flax, hemp, and cotton were all grown in Palestine. The flax was of high quality and was in great demand abroad. Henna and saffron were also exported.

Olive oil, one of the staples of life everywhere in the ancient world, was not much exported from Gaza since Palestine as a whole was not able to produce a surplus of this important commodity.

Gaza was busy with imports as well as with exports. Palestine did not grow enough wheat to satisfy the heavy demand for bread, one of the principal items in the Mediterranean diet, and wheat had to be imported from Cyprus and Egypt. It was shipped in sacks, and when a wheat ship was being unloaded at a quay in Gaza, a steady stream of almost naked men, dusty and sweating under the heavy sacks on their shoulders, made its way up from the holds and down the heavy planks laid between the deck and the quay.

Turning from the cargoes and the quays to the streets, the visitor would find all the activities connected with shipping and trade. The one-story offices, shops, and warehouses, some of cut stone, others of whitewashed mud brick, housed merchants, bankers, chandlers, agents of firms in other ports, and money-lenders. There were ship's carpenters, ropemakers, toolmakers, sailmakers, makers of nets, blacksmiths, and coppersmiths. Early in the morning workmen gathered in the public square waiting to be hired—stevedores, caulkers, unemployed sailors. Everywhere there were wine shops and taverns, with a counter opening directly onto the street, to serve as a bar, and with tables within for people who wished to sit down.

The people who filled the streets about the harbor were a living embodiment of all the varied life of the world of that day. Their dress alone showed their origins and their callings. The sailors, with their short tunics, drawers tucked up about their thighs, and bare feet, looked as sailors had looked for centuries. Workmen hurried about in tunics and short kilts, reaching to above the knee, which were of cotton in the summer and wool in the winter. Merchants and other men of dignified station wore longer robes reaching to the ankles, sometimes plain, sometimes ornamented with embroidery. Foreign visitors could be identified by their exotic garments, and here and there in the crowd one saw African slaves whose wealthy owners dressed them in handsome liveries, brightly colored tunics trimmed with gold or silver braid and buttons. Soldiers and sailors wore uniform tunics bearing imperial emblems, the soldiers' dress varying in color according to the arm of the service to which they

42

belonged—infantry, cavalry, artillery. Bearded Oriental camel drivers in turbans and long, brightly colored robes walked about gazing at the sights of the city. The children, who played everywhere in the streets, wore every variety of costume, from smaller replicas of their elders' dress, if their parents could afford this, to the scanty and nondescript rags of the really poor.

With all its bustle and prosperity, the seaport of Gaza could not escape the taint of the darker pleasures which from earliest times had clustered around the harbors of the world. At night, brawling and drink turned the unlit streets into places which no respectable citizen would enter, even by moonlight, and the soldiers who acted as police had to move about in squads for their own protection. The harbormaster and the police officials had to be prepared to deal with every type of crime. All this was so much taken for granted in the life of a seaport that Gaza was counted fortunate among ancient cities in that the main part of the city lay inland, separated from the harbor by a distance of some three miles. Thus, like Athens with its harbor at the Peiraeus, Gaza enjoyed all the advantages of being a maritime city, while at the same time it was able to protect itself against some of the worst features of water-front life.

Because of the intervening sand dunes, the main part of the city was not visible from the harbor, and the visitor might be surprised, as he made his way along the road, to discover, as he came within sight of it, that the city was built on a high hill, 150 feet above the surrounding desert. The principal part of the city was surrounded by a wall of heavy masonry, with towers for defense placed at strategic points. But the city had expanded beyond its original elevated site, and there were houses all along the slopes of the hill and on the edges of the surrounding plain.

The region between the sea and the city was a sandy waste in which only occasional clumps of coarse, heavy grass grew. But as he came toward the city, the traveler could understand why there had been a settlement on this spot from ancient times. Though it lay on the edge of the desert, Gaza and its neighborhood were blooming and prosperous. There were wells of fresh water everywhere. Gardens and orchards surrounded the houses, and the profile of the city's buildings was accented by trees growing in the public gardens, in the courtyards of houses, and in the public squares. The whole area looked green and inviting, even in the hottest of the summer months, and the visitor could only marvel at the difference that the presence or absence of water would make in this part of the world.

But even though they were so amply supplied, the people of Gaza knew the value of water too well to let any go to waste, and the wells and fountains were supplemented by innumerable cisterns, both public and private, which caught the rain that fell during the winter rainy season, beginning in October and ending in March. The city was thus able to live through the hot, dry months of the long summer. The city's greatest danger was drought; and lack of rain during the winter would mean the failure of the crops which had been planted in the autumn and would be harvested in the spring and early summer. Mark the Deacon described in vivid detail the supplications of the Christians when a drought had brought on a famine during the life of Bishop Porphyry. When the dryness had continued for some time, the people besought the Bishop to pray for rain. He consented and proclaimed a day of fasting, the indispensable preparation for any such undertaking. At evening the people gathered in the principal church of the city, prepared to keep a vigil of prayer. During the night, thirty prayers for rain were said, besides the singing of psalms and readings from the Scriptures. When it was morning, the people set out, carrying a cross and singing hymns, and made their way to the ancient church which stood to the west of the city. When they came to this church, they said further prayers, then visited the martyr's shrine of Timotheus, where prayers were repeated. Then the people returned to the city, stopping on the way three times to pray. Two hours later, a south wind arose and clouds gathered. There was thunder and lightning, and at last rain fell in great drops like hail. The people fell on each other's necks for joy.

Such was the part that water played in the life of Gaza. The presence of the water, combined with the existence of a harbor at this point, had meant that from earliest times some kind of settlement was necessary at Gaza. An ancient road ran along the coast, a few miles inland from the sea, reaching north into Syria and south into Egypt, connecting the string of historic cities built along the coast, some of them older than their classical names: Seleucia, Laodicea, Aradus, Tripolis, Byblus, Berytus, Sidon, Tyre, Ptolemais, Caesarea, Joppa, Azotus, Ascalon. This road had been traveled since the days before recorded history.

From the mountains of Judaea two more roads ran down to Gaza to form a junction there with the coast road. One was the route from Jerusalem, fifty miles away, the other the caravan route which came from Beersheba, twenty-five miles distant. Thus Gaza, unlike some other ancient cities, had never needed to be founded —it had always existed. Its life had always centered about its roads and its harbor.

The climate of that area of Palestine assured Gaza of all the pleasures and advantages of the outdoor life of the Mediterranean world. The winter rains, while sometimes heavy, were not continuous, and there were intervals of bright clear weather almost every day. There was little difference in temperature between day and night during the winter, and since frost and snow were practically unknown, one could live comfortably with only a charcoal brazier to heat the house.

During the summer, the midday heat was intense, but a drop in the temperature at night brought relief and the presence of the sea kept the temperature lower than that of the desert inland. As often in lands where there is no snow, all the houses had flat roofs on which it was agreeable to sleep during the summer.

Thus the life of Gaza, like the life of all Mediterranean cities, was essentially an outdoor life. Daily tasks and social intercourse were carried on, as far as was possible, in the streets or the courtyards of houses, whose living rooms were built about an open area, paved with stone or tile in the well-to-do houses. Here the well stood, and often there was a small garden with a pool and one or two fruit trees. Many gardens had shady outdoor rooms formed by training grape or rose vines over trellises. During the day and into the evening, all family activities were carried on in these pleasant courtyards.

The shops were planned for the same open-air life, all of them opening directly onto the street. Some had counters on which goods were displayed; in others there was simply a large open front in which goods were laid out on the ground and craftsmen sat all day, busy with their work. The merchants and artisans engaged in the same activities tended to group themselves together, and the prospective buyer could walk down a whole street of shoemakers or another street of weavers and dyers, or a third street of coppersmiths, whose metal came from the mines of Sinai. Houses and shops were built sometimes of mud brick, sometimes of stone from the quarries not far from the city. Wood was not plentiful, and was used with care.

Though it was an ancient Phoenician settlement, Gaza by the early sixth century had been so transformed by its long history as a part of the Graeco-Roman world that it was now essentially one of the Hellenic cities which one found everywhere in the Oriental lands of the Roman Empire, even in Semitic Palestine. The hill on which the city was built was roughly an oblong rectangle. When the site was newly laid out after the Roman occupation of

Syria and Palestine, the streets were planned on the practical Hellenistic gridiron pattern named for the city planner Hippodamus of Miletus, who had originated it. Running at right angles to one another, the two sets of streets crossed at regular intervals, forming oblong city blocks. Certain streets were designed to be wider than the others, and for main thoroughfares there were two great avenues crossing the center of the city from north to south and from east to west, dividing the whole area into four sections. Where these avenues crossed, at the center of the city, they opened out to form the main agora, or market place. The whole pattern was bounded by the city walls, and in each of the four sides of the fortifications there was a gate, at the end of one of the main avenues. The western gate stood at the terminus of the straight road running through the dunes which connected Gaza with the harbor.

Such a city plan was the most convenient and orderly that could be devised. It allowed for even distribution of the sunlight at the different hours of the day, and the streets were so oriented as to make the most of the prevailing breezes. The pattern contrasted strikingly with the narrow, winding streets of the old pre-Greek cities, such as Jerusalem.

A Hellenistic city plan also provided ample opportunities for architectural compositions and elegant decoration. Marble colonnades lined the principal streets, and classical forums, ornamented with handsome marble statues and fountains in architectural settings, were placed at convenient parts of the city. The classical temples of earlier pagan days had disappeared, but the churches which succeeded them were themselves developed out of the same classical tradition. In this climate, public baths were not only sources of daily enjoyment but were essential for good health, and the larger baths, with their libraries, lecture halls, gymnasiums, outdoor athletic grounds, and gardens, formed social and cultural centers. A variety of trees and shrubs everywhere in the city gave shade and offered pleasure to the eye. Roses were common and were carefully cultivated. There were many ornamental trees, such as the date palm, the cypress, the myrtle, and the juniper.

It was a charming setting, prosperous and comfortable. The businessmen, scholars, government officials, and gentlemen of leisure who were to be seen everywhere in the streets, the baths, and the public squares were well fed and prosperous, and their servants and slaves lived in what for them could be called relative comfort.

The streets were filled with bustling life, and at the height of the day's activity, just before noon, the main thoroughfares were crowded with people and animals. Donkeys, camels, and mules, however, were not the only beasts of burden, and porters and servants carried many loads that animals might have carried. Wagons and carriages were not common, though two-wheeled carts were sometimes used to transport such loads as timber and building materials. Servants, carrying baskets and wrapped bundles, hurried about on their masters' errands. Officials and prosperous citizens rode on horseback, a servant running before them with a staff to clear the way. Army officers were distinguished by their white uniform cloaks. Vendors of fruit and vegetables led their heavily loaded donkeys through the streets, calling out their wares.

It was in the streets that the visitor could see most clearly that although Gaza was outwardly a classical *polis*, Greek culture was by no means the only strain in the city's life. For this was, historically, a Semitic land. Many of the prosperous gentlemen who spoke Greek had Semitic features and even Semitic names, or Greek names which were obviously translations from the Semitic. And alongside of them there were clear traces of the old stock. In spite of the Dispersion, some Jews still lived in all the cities of Palestine, engaged in many kinds of trade. Though not on good terms with their Christian neighbors, and suffering from political disabilities and constraints imposed by the imperial government, they nevertheless clung to the cities in which they had been born.

The Jews were not the only ancient strain that one saw in the city. In Gaza, as everywhere in Palestine, one found Samaritans, remnant of an ancient people, now bitterly hostile to both Jews and Christians, who in turn despised the members of this strange nation. The Samaritans had repudiated their Jewish origin and Jewish rites and accepted only the Pentateuch of the Old Testament and the original Mosaic ordinances. At the same time, their worship contained heathen elements which attracted the anger of both Jews and Christians. The

Samaritans lived chiefly in the neighborhood of Mount Gerizin, where they had been allowed to build a temple in Hellenistic times, but colonies of them could be found in all the major cities of Palestine. In a city such as Gaza they were a constant source of friction and the municipal authorities watched them carefully, for there were periodic uprisings in which the Samaritans, whipped up by nationalist demagogues, set out to massacre their Christian neighbors and destroy Christian churches.

But if its racial composition was mixed, Gaza was thoroughly Greek in its public pleasures, for these entertainments had been an integral part of the Greek culture brought to these lands by Alexander the Great and his successors. Horse races were one of the most popular sports, and the hippodrome was a center of social life. The theater supplied other pleasures. The tragedies and comedies of the classical dramatic poets were no longer presented regularly on the stage, though they were carefully studied in the schools and famous passages were learned by heart. To take their place, however, there was a flourishing ballet, based upon the well-known stories of mythology. Pantomime, once popular, had degenerated and had become so objectionable that performances had recently been forbidden throughout the Empire by imperial decree. Another old form of entertainment, the hunting and slaying of wild animals in the arena, had likewise had to be forbidden.

If these were the ordinary entertainments in the world of the time, there were other less frequent sources of amusement and refreshment which were more spectacular and more varied. Every city of any significance in the Greek East had throughout its history had a series of festivals, celebrated annually, or sometimes less frequently, which combined athletic contests with musical and literary exhibitions. Some of these had been founded by imperial grants; others had been endowed by wealthy citizens. Athletes, musicians, and men of letters came together to display their skills. The literary men and musicians performed or declaimed their own compositions or offered dramatic recitations or competed in rhetorical contests in which the participants spoke on a set theme.

Since the events took place out of doors, the festivals were held in the summer, when the weather was fine and there was no chance of rain. Many of the gatherings drew large crowds. Everyone in the city would attend, plus numbers of visitors from other cities who enjoyed the opportunity to visit another place—and incidentally to do some shopping. One of the most famous of such festivals was the Olympic games of Antioch, named for the original Olympic games of Greece and celebrated, like the original contests, every four years.

Gaza possessed its full share of such exhibitions, and crowds came to them from all over the Graeco-Roman world to applaud the brilliant literary performances of the local men of letters, whose talents had made them famous throughout the world. The imperial government considered the festivals at Gaza to be so important that the cost of presenting them was subsidized by the imperial treasury.

The merchants took advantage of the influx of visitors and set up fairs at which all manner of luxury goods, both local and imported, were offered. These fairs were famous, and they sometimes were almost as much of an attraction for visitors as the festivals themselves.

So much for the pleasures of the city. How were its mundane affairs regulated?

It was in the hands of the well-to-do citizens that the responsibility for the security and good order of the city rested. The municipal government of a city such as Gaza represented a long tradition in the Roman Empire in which local administration and centralized control were combined in a curious way.

Every city had to pay taxes for both national and local expenses. There had to be revenue to support the imperial government, the elaborate civil service, the army and navy, in addition to the local municipal activities and services, such as the maintenance of the public water supply and the sewers, the provision of public entertainments, the control of standard weights and fair prices in the shops and markets, provision for the police and the fire department. There were public physicians for those unable to pay for private treatment, and both the government and the Church maintained hospitals, orphanages, guesthouses, and homes for elderly people.

While the imperial bureaucracy attended to the collection of some of the revenue necessary for all these varied purposes, it had long been a tradition that some of these services would be provided by wealthy and public-spirited citizens, serving in turn and spending their private fortunes for the benefit of their fellow citizens. Their reward was the prestige they enjoyed, and the honorific inscriptions and statues set up in their honor by the public authorities.

With such a tradition, the great cities of the Graeco-Roman world produced a succession of wealthy and philanthropic families who used their fortunes to build churches, public baths, covered colonnades in the parks, and public fountains. Often they provided the communion silver for use in the churches, sending to Antioch or Constantinople, the great centers of silversmithing, for the pieces, which were then inscribed with their names, and a church might possess a handsome set of these eucharistic vessels, offered by successive generations of the same family.

The sons of such houses were trained from boyhood to expect responsibility and to look forward to taking their places in the public life of their cities. In the early years of the sixth century, two brothers were at the same time serving Gaza in its highest posts, one as bishop of the city, the other as head of the civil administration. Both spent their fortunes freely for the adornment of the city, and the bishop paid for repairing the city walls and improving the towers and the moat.

But the number of families who could bear such expenditures was naturally limited, and some families attempted benefactions they could not really afford. Inevitably, in time, the burdens of public service no longer fell equally, and some of the traditional expenditures had become so great in the latter days of the Roman Empire that the wealthy citizens were no longer able to support these demands, so that the government had had to take over some of the public services which had formerly been in the hands of the local magnates. From time to time, too, unusual military expenses, connected with new campaigns or invasions by foreign powers, made special levies necessary.

Paying taxes was never enjoyable, but the public economy, while often heavily burdened, continued to function and there were always people who managed to become wealthy, though the means they employed were not always to be commended. Commercial circles in Gaza naturally included businessmen of all kinds, and if some of them were honest and others of doubtful character, Gaza was no different in this respect from other cities of its day.

In the economy of that time, subject as it was to inflation, unexpected taxation, and irregular business cycles, the best investment for capital was in land and in shipping. Manufacturing was not centralized, but was carried on through piecework and family enterprise. Land was a safer investment, and shipping, while the risks were high, brought very high returns. If the principles of economics and of government finance were not always well understood, trade in Gaza was prosperous, and not only prosperous in general, but sufficiently flourishing to encourage the development in the city of the intellectual and cultural activity that can best develop against a background of business prosperity.

In the ancient order of things, however, the stable

world based on successful commercial enterprise existed
—indeed was expected to exist—in the midst of quite another world: the world of poverty, of continual unem-
ployment, of illiteracy, disease, and exploitation. The
medical profession was still limited in what it could
accomplish. The slaves of the wealthy houses were often
much better off than the poor freemen. The poor and the
maimed, the halt and the blind, were familiar sights in
the streets of every city and village.

To the people of those times, this did not necessarily
seem to be a defect in the scheme of things. A striking
contrast between wealth and poverty, such as had always
been characteristic of the world of Greece and Rome,
was taken for granted as a natural feature of life. As far
back as Aristotle, Greek thinkers had believed and
taught that men were not created equal by nature. On the
contrary, some were born to rule, others to be ruled; and
those whose lack of natural endowments condemned
them to be the workers and the servants were rendered
incapable, by their circumstances in life, of being educated. It was not proper for them to aspire to a higher
place in the world. It was both necessary and expedient,
Aristotle wrote in his treatise on *Politics*, that there
should be both ruling and ruled elements in nature and
in the animal world. The worker was an instrument of
the economy and it was necessary for such people to
exist and to remain in their intended places.

Poverty, then, with its accompaniment of disease and
crime, was a daily spectacle everywhere in Gaza. The
writer of Proverbs had summed up the experience of the

whole ancient world: "The rich man's wealth is his strong city: the destruction of the poor is their poverty."

Before the advent of Christianity, the imperial government had not done a great deal to remedy the chronic poverty and unemployability of so many of its people. There were, to be sure, free doles of bread and circuses in Rome; there were some free hospitals and, in some places, public physicians paid by the state who gave their services free of charge, but none of this had any bearing on the causes of poverty. There was, for example, no free public education, so that illiteracy continued to be an accepted feature of existence, and the poor boy who could not read or write had no chance of improving his lot. Industry and agriculture were not organized and regulated in such a way that production and employment would be increased. The poor had to do the best they could for themselves.

Christianity had been able to accomplish much with its organized charity, and although the Church had not been able to put an end to the problem of poverty, Christian charity and benevolence had been one of the major factors in the early spread of that faith. The churches in every city became the centers for the distribution of assistance of all kinds: food, clothing, money, social help. In times of famine or earthquake, the churches offered relief to pagans and Christians alike, an action that attracted notice in a world in which the parable of the good Samaritan was a novelty. The pagans indeed endeavored to counteract the success of the Christians by instituting organized charity of their own.

In Gaza, the churches did what they could among the poor, as their means allowed. There was sometimes difficulty in persuading the well-to-do Christians to make sufficient contributions for these purposes, and the priests had to be skilled in knowing how to approach the members of their congregations. One benefaction was well known, namely the endowment established by Bishop Porphyry in his will, which provided for the payment of a small sum to each poor person in the city during Lent.

But for all its good will, the Church had not the means to accomplish everything. Indeed, it had to accept some of the customs it found. Unable to put an end to slavery, which was one of the bases of the ancient economy, the Church itself had ended by owning slaves. St. Paul's injunctions to slaves and masters to remember their obligations to one another doubtless accomplished some good.

So there were in Gaza, as elsewhere, two worlds—the world of the grinding struggle for existence and the world of festivals, education, and leisure; the world of the Semitic-speaking people who lived and died in the streets of Gaza, as their forebears had done, back to the days of the Philistines, and the world of the Greek-speaking high officials and scholars whose careers rotated about the poles of Constantinople and Alexandria and the glittering society of the most powerful empire on earth; the world of the people who lived in mud hovels and ate scraps of bread and pulse and olives—or, if they could not get this, garbage—and the world of the well-

58

to-do who gathered in elegant dining rooms whose mosaic floors illustrated the celebrated episodes of Greek mythology, sometimes some of the rather naughty episodes.

III.

The City's Neighbors

Thou visitest the earth and waterest it.
—Psalm LXV

The traveler in the Holy Land who climbed Mount Quarantana might not see "all the kingdoms of the world in a moment of time," as Jesus is said to have done when according to tradition He was tempted on that mountain, but he would have a magnificent view of Jericho and of the Fords of the Jordan, a green and fertile oasis whose richness stood out the more strikingly against the somber brown and gray of the surrounding desert. In this picture the traveler could see the contrast between the city and the country, between the desert and the sown, which affected, directly or indirectly, human life and activities in all of Palestine.

There was no mountain near Gaza, but the city itself was sufficiently elevated above the surrounding plain to make it possible for one who climbed to the ramparts of the city wall to command a good view of the surrounding countryside, green and fertile, thanks to the springs and wells which were to be found throughout this area on the edge of the desert.

Here, indeed, was an essential part of the life of the city; for if man was, as Aristotle wrote, "by nature an animal intended to live in a city," he was also an animal who must eat. In the early sixth century, the time had not yet come when an abundant and varied supply of food at all times could be taken for granted as a normal part of city life. The important cities, and those which were especially blessed in their situations, did have enough food in ordinary times; but even they had to eat what the various seasons of the year produced, and they had to live with only a limited margin of reserves. In the world of that day, the production, storage, and transportation of food presented problems for which there were no remedies then available.

A visitor to Gaza could see that the life of the farmers in the neighborhood of the city was much like that of all the peasants whose lot it was to live near the great cities of the Empire and supply the means of their daily sustenance. There was, to begin with, a contrast in language and race. If Gaza was historically an old Philistine city, it was now a metropolis in which the principal language was Greek, supplemented by Latin and the various tongues spoken by sailors and traders. If there were any descendants of the Philistines left in the city, they now spoke Greek or perhaps Aramaic.

In the country it was different. Many of the peasants

were of Jewish blood, some doubtless had Philistine blood, but they all represented an occupation of the land, in the farmer's unceasing toil, that went back to the days of Samson and beyond. Language might change, religion might change, as one power or another won control of the area, but the farmers continued their work, successive generations living in the same spot and laboring with tools and methods that in most cases had not changed for centuries. The masters of the city to whom the farmers took their products might be in turn Egyptian, Philistine, Israelite, Macedonian, or Roman (the Roman occupation was itself only a relatively small part of the history of these lands). The gardens, vineyards, orchards and pastures produced the same food, which the farmers carried into the city on camels and donkeys whose lineage was as old as theirs.

A few of the larger farms, owned by more prosperous or more fortunate folk, had their own farmhouses surrounded by barns and stables. The whole complex was enclosed within a mud-brick wall for protection against thieves and against the traveling bands of brigands and of the Samaritans, who periodically raided their Christian neighbors. For the most part, however, the farmers lived in little villages grouped along the main roads, the houses huddled together for protection, with a village square and a small church as the centers of community life. There were many of these villages throughout Palestine, and life in them had not changed essentially from the days of the New Testament, in which one could see homely pictures of the daily life of the peasants.

The life was monotonous, wholly concerned with the production of food. From his mud-brick house, with its little courtyard attached for domestic animals, the farmer and such of his family as could work with him would set out before daylight for the fields around the village in which he labored. If he were lucky, the farmer owned his own fields. But if bad luck had come upon him —a succession of poor crops, a visitation of locusts, a series of droughts, or one of the varieties of insect pests —the farmer might have lost his land, through mortgage or even forced sale, to one of the wealthy magnates who lived in Gaza and possessed enough capital to survive the emergencies and enough political influence (and the ability to pay the right bribes) to deal with the corrupt tax collectors, whose rapacity the little farmer by himself could not withstand. A tax collector was permitted, by the terms of his contract, to keep for himself anything above the legal amount that he could extort, and a farmer would be helpless, especially when the tax collector literally carried a big stick. Even if crops had failed and the farmer had made no money, the taxes were still exacted, and this was one of the major reasons why so many farms, their owners ruined, had come into the hands of the wealthy landowners in the cities, who often owned whole villages with their surrounding lands.

Aristotle, in his treatise on *Politics,* had, as was traditional, pronounced that the agricultural life promoted solid virtues. Industry, frugality, and freedom from covetousness were, the philosopher pointed out, the qualities one would look for in a farmer or shepherd, and his life in the open air should give him a robust physique. But Aristotle did not have occasion to note that over against these advantages the agricultural life was exposed to a number of hazards that had impelled many people to flee from the land and seek a living in the cities—where they often discovered that they could not get beyond the crowd of the chronically unemployed, who were a normal feature of life in every large city.

The work on the land was, indeed, infinitely laborious, as it had been for centuries. Plowing was done with a very simple (and not very efficient) wooden plow, tipped with iron, drawn sometimes by one ox, sometimes by two oxen. Some farmers employed an ox and an ass yoked together. As in the famous parable, sowing was done by hand, and much seed was inevitably wasted. Reaping was likewise hand labor, with a primitive sickle. Grain was threshed outdoors on a hard floor, the wind carrying away the chaff. Often the winnowing was done by night, when, in the climate of Palestine, there was more wind. The grain was thrown into the air with a large fan, and when it had been winnowed, it was collected into barns or sometimes underground pits.

To the constant round of labor were added the hazards of nature, hazards such as had always plagued the country people of the ancient world. It is only surprising that the ancient world was able to live as well as it did. With no knowledge of the chemistry of the soil and only the most primitive natural fertilizers, a farmer might find his land much less productive than it should have been. Rotation of crops was imperfectly understood and not widely used. Land that had become exhausted simply had to be abandoned.

The possible misfortunes were numerous. Droughts had to be expected, and in a land such as Palestine, with a long, rainless summer, there was always the question of how much water it was possible to catch and store in pits and cisterns. There was no known remedy against the locusts and the insects that might appear without warning. If an epidemic of disease fell upon the farm animals, land would go out of cultivation because of the loss of the beasts used for plowing.

There were so many things that were terribly familiar to the farmer. Worms might eat the grapes as they ripened on the vines, or a blight might cause the olive trees to drop their fruit. Locusts, if they came, would destroy crops completely, including the seeds which should have been used for future sowing. It was not unknown for a hailstorm to arrive just at the time of the vintage, destroying the grapes and stripping the leaves from the vines. Some farmers could remember watching helplessly as clouds gathered suddenly on a clear day with still air, bringing in a few minutes a storm of the dreaded hail.

Usually the farmer himself had been born on the land, the son of a farmer; people did not leave the cities to seek a living on the land. Sometimes the farmer was a veteran of the imperial army, presented by the government with a small farm at the completion of his term of service. Often such a man might be young enough to marry and start a family, and he might have some agricultural background anyway, for the rural areas were an important source of conscripts for the army and many soldiers were farmers' sons.

As the farmer's children grew up, they had little or no schooling. There was no such opportunity for most country children, unless there was a grandmother living with the family who could herself read and write and thus teach the children, and in this case the children were fortunate indeed. But they had to work hard from the earliest possible age, caring for the younger children, weeding, doing the household chores, tending sheep, or, finally, working in the fields.

For such children the future was not bright. Only a certain number of mouths could be fed with the produce and profit of the average farm. This put a limit on the size of the families, but even so it often proved impossible for young men to stay with their parents' property and in this case the usual choices were service in the army or migration to the "big city," where it often proved less easy to make a living than one had supposed.

Faced with this prospect, some parents sold their children as slaves or to childless couples. Or they could turn to the monastery if there was one near by which was prepared to take charge of children. Palestine was a land of monks and monasteries, and people depended on them for food in emergencies, as well as for religious help. Hence it came that farmers in distress or overburdened with large families would entrust their children to the monks, who would educate them and care for them. When these children came of age, they were allowed to leave if they wished; but they could, if they desired, remain and become monks, and many did. There was a story of an aged monk who had been placed in a monastery at the age of three and had never stepped outside it. As a very old man, he told a visitor he had no idea what a pig or a rooster looked like.

There were certain areas of the Empire in which there were enormous estates, worked by gangs of slaves or by tenant farmers. Such could be found in Anatolia and Syria, and there had been many in North Africa and Italy before the barbarian invasions. Some were owned by the government, some by great landlords who lived in Constantinople or Antioch and only visited their lands occasionally. These estates had only a very distant connection with the city civilization they helped to support, and the slaves and peasants knew of these great cities only in the vaguest way; certainly they never expected to see them.

In the case of a city such as Gaza, however, the farmer's role was quite different. For one thing, the area that could supply the city directly was very well defined. According to immemorial custom, the farmer took his produce to the city himself, sometimes daily, sometimes once a week, on market day—depending on how much time he could spare from his work—and he had to be able to make the round trip in one day. He would set out, sometimes before daylight, accompanied by some or all of his family, with the goods to be sold loaded on camels or donkeys. Progress along the dusty roads was necessarily slow, even slower, of course, if there were livestock (such as sheep or pigs) to be driven on foot. Then, after he had sold his goods in the city market or hawked them along the streets, the farmer liked to be able to get back to his house before dark, for there might be robbers along the road, on the lookout for the money the farmer had received in the city. The return journey might be as slow as the morning trip, for the municipal authorities, when necessary, forced the farmers to allow their beasts to be loaded with debris of building operations or other refuse which had to be carried out of the city.

Of course there were other sources of food supply for a city such as Gaza. Wheat, for the bread which had always been a staple of the Mediterranean diet, might be brought from Egypt by sea; there was fish, dried or fresh, at the city's doorstep (though the poor could not afford it), and wine and dried fruit, if not produced locally, might be brought from the interior of Palestine by caravan. Still, most of the fresh food was brought to the city, on a daily or weekly basis, by the farmer who had grown it or the fisherman who had caught it; and the housewife or kitchen servant who was going to cook the food bought it, most often, directly from the farmer or fisherman. A middleman was not necessary, and the city dweller lived in very close touch with the source of his daily diet.

The farmer and the fisherman and their customers in the city lived totally different kinds of lives. Their culture was totally different, often their language as well. If their religion was the same, at least nominally, in origin and descent they represented different threads of history. It was food that was their common denominator, and the most patrician family in Gaza was directly dependent for its supply of such everyday things as cucumbers upon the farmer who had grown them and then had walked, perhaps for two or three hours, to bring them into the city.

In the everyday life of Gaza, the supply of cucumbers was enjoyed without much thought, but the directness of this dependence of the city on its lands might become suddenly and sharply clear if there were a drought or other disaster of nature. If the crops failed, the farmer—if he were fortunate—could hoard a supply of his own produce for his own use or for speculation as prices in the city rose. During a famine, people from the city would often go out into the country looking for food, and a lucky farmer might have handsome profits. But if the drought were severe, or prolonged, the farmer might in the end be no better off than anyone else; for in the case of a local crop failure of serious proportions it was extremely difficult—sometimes, indeed, impossible—for the authorities to import food from other areas which had not been affected. Transportation of bulky cargoes by sea was possible and might not be too expensive, and here a place such as Gaza, close to the sea, was lucky. But to transport by land a heavy and bulky commodity such as wheat was extremely expensive if any distance were involved, and it was well known that there had been historic occasions when it had literally been impossible to send adequate relief to regions which had been stricken with famine.

A prolonged crop failure and scarcity of food would set off a price spiral of unlimited potential. When wheat, for example, became scarce, the farmers and the merchants in the cities stopped selling it and held their stocks against a further rise in prices. The wealthy and the speculators, with sufficient capital and sufficient reserves of food at their command, bought all the wheat they could, even at high prices, in the expectation of a further rise. If, as happened on occasion, the authorities intervened and attempted to fix prices, the merchants simply went out of business, waiting for a return of normal times. This meant profits for some, starvation for others; and farmers, fishermen, and city workmen would starve together.

Here—quite aside from the human suffering, which in those days was taken for granted as a part of the natural order of things—there could be a real dislocation of the local economy. The city-country economy was simple and on a relatively small scale, but it depended on regular exchange and it could easily be upset. The providing of food, necessary for the physical life of the city, was only one transaction in the economic exchange. The farmer in fact depended entirely on his sales in the city for the cash which was necessary to pay his taxes to the tax collector stationed in the village. Many of the simple goods the farmer needed—cloth, shoes, earthenware household utensils, and so on, were made in his village and could be obtained by bartering food; but there were other articles he could usually obtain only in the city—

rope, tools, harness, metalware, and so on—and here the economy was a cash economy, for the city merchants could not do business wholly on barter. Thus a city such as Gaza possessed a number of artisans and craftsmen whose principal function in the economy was to supply the farmers with the products of their workshops. The amount of money that circulated in a local economy of this kind was relatively small, but many people in the city depended upon this for their living, quite as much as the farmers did, and any stoppage could mean personal disaster for these humble citizens of the great Empire.

Was the dichotomy of culture between city and country a natural development, to be accepted and regarded, if not as praiseworthy, at least not as blameworthy? Was the elegant gentleman of Gaza, living in a fine house, bathing in a luxurious public bath, strolling in the colonnades of the main street, conscious that the money he was spending for a new book, such as he might buy any day without a second thought, was the equivalent of a week's income or more for a farmer and his family?

Probably neither the gentleman nor the farmer would have seen anything incongruous in the difference. It was a part of the order of nature. The Empire was composed of a series of great cities, standing alone as relatively tiny concentrations of humanity surrounded by great expanses of land, sometimes cultivated, sometimes waste or forest. Were the people in the cities aware that nothing had ever been done to bring country folk into the sphere of city civilization? Had anything ever been done—

should anything be done—to give the farmer at least some of the social and intellectual benefits developed out of the civilization of Athens?

This was a thought that would have occurred neither to the citizen nor to the peasant, and surely no one would have thought it a failure of the city if the countryside lived a totally different life, almost in a different world. This was not the concern of the city; the countryside was not a part of its social and intellectual mission. Men were made for different stations in life—Aristotle had said it —and a man was fortunate if he knew his station and accepted it in the proper spirit.

The farmer, prodding his donkeys with a sharpened stick as he took his melons and grapes to market in Gaza, had never heard of Aristotle.

IV.

Things Temporal and Things Eternal

*The ruler is sovereign over all; but he is also,
along with all, the servant of God.*
—AGAPETUS, *Address to Justinian*

AN IMPERIAL COURIER, traveling at top speed with an urgent message, needed eleven or twelve days to cover the nine hundred miles between Gaza and Constantinople, even with all the resources of the imperial post. The sea voyage might take twenty days or even longer if winds were not favorable. Yet Gaza, like every city of the great Empire, lived in the shadow of Constantinople.

It might represent the situation more correctly to say that the cities lived in the shadow of the emperor—and of the imperial court. The emperor indeed made himself felt everywhere in his realm.

In an empire without a written constitution, the sovereign was bound to be looked upon as the symbol of the powers and functions of the state; and when, in addition, the democratic tradition of participation by people in their government had disappeared, the monarch became not only the symbol but the embodiment of the life of the state.

The Roman emperor had been an absolute ruler in effect since the time of Diocletian (A.D. 284–305). Subsequent emperors were heirs of the absolute powers that Diocletian had thought it necessary to take upon himself in order to stabilize the state. In addition, the successors had come to take on a new area of responsibility unknown to Diocletian and his predecessors, that of head of the Church. With the conversion to Christianity of Constantine the Great, it became necessary to understand and define the relationship to the Church of a traditionally absolute monarch who in the existing political theory reigned under the protection of one of the great pagan deities. If pagan monarchs had been looked upon as fathers, guardians, and protectors of their people and as good shepherds of their subjects, appointed to office by the will of the supreme ruler of the universe, it was only natural that the monarch of an empire in which the Church was emancipated and promoted to the official religion should be given a role of authority and responsibility in connection with the Church.

Thus it was that in the brightness of the new era, Eusebius of Caesarea, the learned and accomplished scholar and bishop, Constantine's personal adviser and guide in religious matters, provided the new political theory of the powers and responsibilities of the new Christian Roman emperor, divinely appointed successor to the old pagan emperor. Eusebius' theory brought together the various strands of traditional conceptions of the ruler on which society had been built in Rome and the Hellenistic world and in earlier times. The Christian Roman emperor ruled by divine choice, God having in unseen fashion arranged for his earthly promotion. The emperor was guided by messages transmitted to him from on high, and he was responsible to God for the spiritual well-being of his subjects. He was in fact God's vicegerent on earth, carrying out in the mundane sphere functions corresponding to those of God in heaven.

Hence the power and authority of the emperor were above any question: they were divine in origin and impulse. Traditionally the ruler had been Law Incarnate, and his spoken word represented the divine power by which he ruled. It was a tremendous sanction, but it was at the same time a tremendous responsibility, for the emperor was accountable to God for his actions and for the material and spiritual prosperity and safety of the state.

Between the inaugural age of Constantine and the early sixth century there had been a succession of emperors, men of every sort, brought to the throne sometimes by hereditary succession or appointment, more often through election by the army and by the senate, which survived as a figurehead. As the new imperial power was established, there grew up an expanded form of the traditional imperial bureaucracy upon which the complicated administrative life of the state depended. The ancient functions of the municipalities and the provinces gradually dwindled and the central government became more and more powerful. Inevitably there was venality and corruption; but the bureaucratic machine worked about as well as could be expected in that time.

The dominant characteristic of the bureaucracy was that it was the personal instrument of the emperor. The emperor himself controlled and directed it through the heads of departments and chiefs of bureaus in Constantinople, but even here his power was unlimited, for on occasion it was his privilege to go over the head of a superior official and deal directly with a subordinate. The whole civil service was organized along military lines and the officials wore uniforms and insignia of rank. The portfolio, or *mappa,* was a badge of membership in the civil service, and a symbolic portfolio was actually embroidered on the front of the official's tunic, in the position in which a real portfolio would have been carried in the right hand.

Being the personal instrument and direct representative of the emperor, the bureaucratic official was the embodiment of the emperor's absolute power. Every official, from the great praetorian prefects in Constantinople to the lowliest tax clerk in a village on the edge of the desert in Egypt, was a direct personal extension of the imperial power. Through his officials, it was said, the emperor was present everywhere in his realm, and his officials served as his eyes and ears. Every official in Gaza was the direct agent of the emperor.

An even more concrete symbolism of the sovereign's role was also present everywhere, in the form of the imperial portraits. These were official portraits, painted on

wood or sculptured in marble or bronze, which were prepared in Constantinople immediately on the accession
of a new emperor and dispatched to all government
offices throughout the Empire. On the analogy of the
statues of the pagan gods in the classical era, the power
of the ruler was conceived to reside in the image. Oaths
were sworn in front of the portraits, and as a judge sat
beneath the effigy of the sovereign, the sentence he pronounced was spoken in the emperor's name. Every official transaction took place in the presence of the portrait. Any kind of disrespect or insult offered to the
portrait constituted *laesa maiestas*.

Such was the figure of the emperor as it made itself
felt throughout the realm. What was the response to it
by the people of the Empire, specifically by the people of
Gaza and of Palestine?

In order to understand how the subjects felt, it is necessary to know something of the Empire and of its
growth.

The Roman Empire in the early years of the sixth century, extending over the eastern end of the Mediterranean Basin, was not a homogeneous state, racially, lin-
guistically, or culturally. Rome had become the leading
world state only after a number of other states had
reached their apogees and declined. Babylonia, Assyria,
Persia, Egypt, Greece, the Macedonia of Alexander the
Great, the Hellenistic kingdoms, Israel—all had flourished before Rome rose to power and occupied their
lands. The Romans did not attempt to obliterate the existing cultures in the lands they occupied, nor was any

attempt made to assimilate the native populations to Roman culture. Some individuals, for their own practical ends, Romanized themselves, but these were exceptions. Left to speak their own languages and carry on their own civilizations, the indigenous peoples inevitably looked upon the Romans as an occupying power, alien in many respects. The new Graeco-Roman world flourished, but beneath it there was an older world which could only live with its conquerors on terms of tolerance at the best, hostility at the worst.

The coming of Christianity did indeed provide a bond that drew together at least some sections of the heterogeneous peoples of the Empire. But it did not prove to be a bond that supplanted the elements of diversity. Ancient language and race, and the instinctive distrust of the foreigner which had been developed in mankind before the advent of Christianity, proved too strong. When with the emancipation of Christianity in the early fourth century increased theological study produced serious differences of opinion, these quickly became matters of public concern. It was easy for the differences, in the hands of demagogues, to pass beyond the purely religious concern and become burning questions related to the latent hostility and suppressed nationalism of the various parts of the Empire. One could hate the foreigner more vehemently if he represented a threat to one's religious convictions.

By the early years of the sixth century, Gaza, being in Palestine, was in a center of religious-nationalistic dissension. The situation had grown out of the protracted

78

theological debates over the nature of Christ. Whether the Savior was both human and divine at once or whether He was a primarily human or a primarily divine figure was a matter of the most urgent importance, for on it depended one's conception of the nature of the salvation He offered. If Christ united within Himself both a human nature and a divine nature, one could believe that God had become incarnate in human form in order to bring salvation to mankind in the shape of a Person that mankind could understand, with which, under the human aspect, mankind could feel a bond. But if it were denied that one person could unite within himself both a human and a divine nature—and there were people who felt bound to deny this—then the salvation that was offered had to be different.

What emerged from this debate in the early part of the sixth century was two opposing camps, one centered on Constantinople, the other on Alexandria and Antioch. The imperial capital represented the orthodox, who upheld the dual nature of Christ. But in Syria, Palestine, and Egypt, the old home of Semitic monotheism, many people—coming finally to be the majority—felt that the orthodox definition of the dual nature of the Savior entailed a diminution of His divinity and constituted a threat to the true understanding of the nature of the incarnate deity. Called the Monophysites because they insisted upon the oneness of the divine nature in Christ, these dissidents from the orthodox definition kept up a vigorous opposition to the theology of the imperial capital, and when on occasion the authorities in Constantinople attempted to suppress them by force, there was rioting and bloodshed in the streets of Alexandria and Antioch and in the other cities and towns where the two theologies clashed.

The course of the struggle was uneven, depending upon the fortunes of the leaders on either side, and Gaza, like all other large centers, witnessed these vicissitudes in its own ecclesiastical community. In a state such as the Roman Empire, much could depend upon the personal inclination of the emperor. In the conservative and traditional atmosphere of Constantinople, the emperors had long been orthodox. But a great change occurred when the chances of political life in the capital brought to the throne the experienced treasury official Anastasius (A.D. 491–518). Anastasius had Monophysite sympathies, and during his reign the fortunes of the dissidents rose. It was an imperial prerogative to influence the selection of candidates when an episcopal throne became vacant, and it would not be long before the bishoprics in Egypt, Palestine, and Syria were occupied by Monophysites. The imperial system being what it was, however, a policy of this kind could not be maintained permanently, and the death of Anastasius brought to the throne the orthodox Justin I (A.D. 518–527), who was shortly succeeded by his vigorously orthodox nephew Justinian (A.D. 527–565). With the accession of Justin, the Monophysite bishops were swept off into exile and replaced by selected orthodox prelates.

If there were complaints from some quarters that the emperors sometimes interfered in the internal affairs of the Church, it could be answered that it was the emperor's duty to watch over the spiritual life of his subjects and make certain that they held the True Faith, which alone could assure their salvation and a blessed life after death. Religious dissension threatened not only the spiritual life but the material prosperity and political stability of the state, and it was the duty of the emperor to enforce orthodox belief—by force if necessary. The emperor was obliged by his duties to take all necessary measures to eradicate pagans, Jews, and Samaritans, and all such dissident groups began to experience real persecution at the accession of Justinian. The unity and security of the state was involved.

This, then, was the picture of the emperor in the minds of the people of Gaza, orthodox and Monophysite. It was the only way of life that any of them had known, and it was the inevitable framework of life in a city of the Empire in those days. And it was not exclusively a feature of city life. If anything, religious partisanship was stronger in the countryside by reason of the age-old conservatism of the agricultural folk, strengthened by their lack of contact with the people of the city.

V

The World of the Mind

*"No, but really, my good Adeimantus, we are not laying upon
the Guardians a whole number of burdensome duties, as you
might suppose. It will be easy enough, if only they will see to
'the one great thing,' as the saying goes, though I would rather
call it the one thing that is sufficient: education and nurture.
If a sound education has made them reasonable men, they will
easily see their way through all these matters."*
—PLATO, *Republic*

IT IS MUCH TO BE DOUBTED that the well-educated and
socially and economically secure citizens of Gaza realized that the intellectual and cultural advantages they
enjoyed were possessions that were not necessarily to be
taken for granted. Most probably they gave no thought
to the fact that their less fortunate brothers, the unedu-
cated poor, were not concerned with such matters of the
intellect and the emotions. Certainly in many cases the
poor did not even know that such things existed, or if
they did know of them, their understanding of them was
very imperfect indeed. Probably not all of the humble
folk of Gaza had any clear idea who Pontius Pilate was,
and if they did not know what his famous question had
been, this was hardly something that concerned people
to whom it was a harsh struggle merely to maintain life.

But people who had education and leisure were very much concerned with such things, and Pilate's question, or something like it, was in their minds, consciously or unconsciously.

How, then, had the cultivated citizens of Gaza come to possess the intellectual equipment they enjoyed? Were they really aware of what an astonishing achievement their mental capacities and curiosities represented?

In classical times, before the coming of Christianity, the thinkers of Greece—scientists, philosophers, poets, dramatists, historians—had spent their lives in the study of man. Man was the center of the universe. Sophocles had spoken for all Greek intellectuals when he wrote the famous chorus of the *Antigone*:

Wonders are many, and nothing is more wonderful than a man.

This creature passes over even the gray sea
in the winter storms,

Making his way over the billows which break about him.

He vexes the earth, the oldest of the gods, ageless and unwearying . . . .

He snares the race of lighthearted birds

And the tribes of savage beasts and the creatures that live in the sea . . . .

He learned speech, and thought

Which is swift as the wind, and the laws of life in cities.

He no longer lodges out of doors, having to flee frost and rain.

Fertile in all resources, he approaches nothing in the future without resources.

83

Only from Death he shall not achieve escape.
But he has learned to dispel many baffling diseases.

Possessing in his skill wisdom and invention
That go beyond his expectation, sometimes he comes to
    good, sometimes to evil.
If he keeps the laws, and justice sworn to in divine oaths,
He stands high in his city. But that man loses his city
Who dares to dwell with sin . . . .

Every educated man in Gaza was familiar with this
great chorus. Every Christian knew that this ancient
view of man had been replaced by the Divine Word,
which taught that man was the child of God. Yet the
history of Greek intellectual activity was to a large extent the history of the study of man and of all that per-
tained to him; and if the truth had come with Christianity, there was still something to be learned from the
studies of the earlier Greek thinkers.

Six hundred years after the birth of Christ, human
knowledge, in Gaza and in the other cities of the Graeco-
Roman world, had advanced to the point at which the
humble and uncertain beginnings of the quest for scientific knowledge were all but forgotten. The earliest
philosophers and scientists were now, for the most part,
only names, yet their work had started the Greek mind
on the path it had followed ever since.

The curiosity and intelligence of the Greek mind, exhibited in such a variety of ways in cities such as Gaza,
Alexandria, Antioch, and Constantinople, had begun to
show itself seven centuries and more before the birth of

Christ. What was man and why did he exist? What was man in nature, and what was nature?

Setting out on these lines of systematic and rational explanation, for the first time in the history of mankind, the Greek thinkers saw their problem under two aspects.

At first it was to the physical world that they devoted themselves. What is the nature of matter? With no instruments or laboratories, the early philosopher-scientists had to seek the answers to their questions solely on the basis of observation and reasoning. A whole series of answers was proposed, each new hypothesis showing that the others had not won unanimous acceptance.

Seeing that the basic materials of the world appeared to be earth, air, fire, and water, Thales of Miletus, early in the sixth century before Christ, concluded that water was the basic substance from which all material things are formed and to which they will revert. It would have been impossible, at that day, to make a physical demonstration of such an idea. The real significance of Thales' thought was that it represented an effort to discover whether there was not some basic principle behind the visible changes we can see in the world. Is there, in fact, some single property or force that gives unity and action to everything that exists?

Other philosophers sought more convincing answers to Thales' question. Anaximander of Miletus worked out a theory of the evolution and adaptation to environment of living creatures. Man, for example, developed ultimately from a fish. Heraclitus of Ephesus, who died only about a century before Aristotle was born, put forward two striking ideas. First, the principle of existence or being is change, "flux," that is, constant motion, constant succession of changes. The most changeable of all the basic elements is fire, and so all things must be composed of fire, or develop out of fire.

Heraclitus' ideas were followed quickly by the hypothesis of Leucippus and Democritus, the fathers of the atomic theory. Still working without scientific instruments or laboratory facilities, Leucippus and Democritus concluded that if one could subdivide physical matter far enough, one must eventually reach units that were in themselves indivisible. These particles were to be called atoms, meaning literally in Greek something that could not be cut. There is actually, the atomists believed, only one kind of atomic substance, out of which the whole world is formed. Material substances are composed of atoms which are perpetually in motion.

The final step in this evolution of scientific thought remained for Anaxagoras, another philosopher of the Ionian coast and the first of the natural scientists to establish himself in Athens. Matter, he concluded, was both uncreated and indestructible; but there must be a moving force behind nature, a force which would account for motion and change and the processes to be observed all about us. This force, Anaxagoras believed, was an abstraction that he called Mind. Mind causes matter to come together to form the world and then controls the world thus formed.

Here was a milestone in human thought, namely the distinction of the visible and the invisible. The idea that

there was an intangible force which governs the visible
world of nature was so much a part of ordinary mental
equipment in the Gaza of the early sixth century that
people seldom stopped to realize the significance of the
step Anaxagoras had been able to take. What would the
Greek world of science, philosophy, and religion have
been without it?

The stage was thus set for the towering achievement
of Aristotle. Convinced that speculation by itself could
not lead to assured knowledge, Aristotle set out to organ-
ize the whole of human knowledge and thought on the
basis of empirical inquiry. He determined that the true
scientist's work must be based on the integration of close
observation with acute reasoning. Aristotle's unique passion for research established a scientific method and scientific standard that was never changed thereafter. An
enormous collection of materials of all kinds was made
the basis of a new science of biology. At the same time,
logical thought was established as a science, forming the
only possible basis for human inquiry. This inquiry ex-
tended into metaphysics, ethics, and politics. In all this
there was Aristotle's special gift, an inspired common
sense, combined with a love of order and tidiness, which
established the working program of scientific thought
for all time. Every philosopher and every scientist who
came after Aristotle was indebted to the Master; but
the Master's spirit had become so much a part of all subsequent thought and investigation that many scientists
and philosophers were unaware of their debt to their
predecessor and simply accepted, without reflection, the

scientific method which took for granted all that Aristotle had had to work out and establish for the first time. Aristotle's work was still available for the student in the early sixth century, and there were many learned commentaries to guide the reader. In the fourth century after Christ, the pagan teacher Themistius had had the happy idea of writing a series of paraphrases of Aristotle's treatises. These were simplified versions, designed to make more readily and more widely accessible the Master's ideas, which were not always easy to follow because they were often closely reasoned and embedded in minute analyses and investigations of detail. Like other ancient writers, Aristotle was unable to make use of the footnote, and this made some of his expositions difficult to follow.

Themistius' paraphrases rendered important service in preserving Aristotle's ideas as a part of the educational tradition; and Themistius' own philosophical and ethical writings, highly appreciated for both style and content, were in part designed to propagate the ethical teachings of Aristotle and Plato.

If Aristotle represented the perfection of scientific method and the apogee of scientific thought, Socrates and Plato represented the second direction taken by Greek speculative thought. Aristotle and his predecessors had carried the investigation of the physical world as far as it could then be taken. But in this physical world there was man. Here was a fascinating subject for study and speculation—and not merely fascinating, indeed, for what was the physical world without man?

Man had long been the theme of poets and dramatists, beginning with Homer. The dramatic poets had made the theater the medium for the study of man's moral problems and for the depiction of his fate in the universe. Aristotle, himself a philosopher and a religious man, had set down, quite simply and a little baldly, the scientist's definition of man: "It is the peculiarity of man, in comparison with the rest of the animal world, that he alone possesses a perception of good and evil, of the just and the unjust, and of other similar qualities; and it is association in a common perception of these things that makes a family and a city." Thus "Man, when perfected, is the best of animals; but if he be isolated from law and justice he is the worst of all."

Aristotle's scientific point of view represented one conception of the nature of man. Another conception had, before Aristotle's time, been developed by Socrates and Plato, who undertook to make man's world of thought and emotion the object of deeper and more creative speculation than any previous Greek thinker had ventured upon. Socrates left no philosophical writings but he lived and spoke in Plato's pages. Here, for the first time, the human soul became a reality, and it was shown to be immortal. It has been said, indeed, that Socrates "discovered the soul." The dignity and the destiny of man became different things after the work of Socrates and his pupil. All this became a part of the heritage of Gaza, as one among the cities of the Christian Empire, for it was clear to Christian thinkers that Plato approximated in many ways to Christian thought. "Our Plato," he had been called by a Christian philosopher, and it was on this basis that he was studied in the schools of Gaza.

Throughout all his works there were pages that showed how far Plato had been able to go, on the basis of human reasoning alone, in the real understanding of man and his soul. Socrates and Cebes, for example, were shown conversing on the destiny of the soul. Socrates spoke:

"But what about the soul, then, the invisible part of us, which goes away to a place like itself, noble, pure and invisible—the unseen world as we rightly call it—and into the presence of the good and wise God, whither, if God wills, my soul must soon go too? Being of such a character and nature as it is, is our soul dispersed and destroyed directly it parts company with the body, as men say? Far from it, my dear Cebes and Simmias, but it is much more like this: if it is pure when it leaves the body it brings nothing of the body away with it, because it did not willingly associate with it in this life but avoided it and kept itself to itself because that was its one aim—but that is nothing else than philosophizing in the proper sense of the word and really studying to die without regret. Or would this not be studying to die?"

"It certainly would."

"Therefore being so situated the soul departs to what is like itself, namely the Unseen, a divine, immortal, and wise place, and when it gets there, it is given to be happy, because it is rid of deceit and foolishness and fears and untamed passions and the other evils that afflict human nature, and as is said of those who have been initiated into the mysteries, it lives for the rest of the time with the gods."

Elsewhere in the same dialogue, Socrates summed up his thoughts on death and the other world:

> "I would be wrong not to resent death, if I did not think that when I die I shall come to other gods both wise and good, and also to men who have died and are better than men here. I assure you that I hope to be with good men, but this I would not positively assert. That I shall go to gods who will be very good masters, I assure you that I should assert as strongly as anything about all this. For that reason I do not to the same extent resent dying, but I have a good hope that something awaits the dead, and according to the old tradition, something much better for the good than for the wicked."

What was reality, and what was truth? For Plato, the question such as that asked by Pilate led to one of the greatest certainties that man could have, namely the existence of an ideal, abstract truth and knowledge, beyond the accidents of the present world, existing forever in its pure form. This was put very simply in one of the dialogues:

> Socrates: "We must say good-bye to individuals and me and Gorgias and Philebus quite firmly, and make a solemn profession of faith to the following effect."
> Protarchus: "To what effect?"
> Socrates: "That the sure and pure and true and unsullied, as we call it, is concerned with what is ever the same without change or mingling of outside elements, or with what is most akin to that. But all else must be reckoned secondary and subordinate."

Protarchus: "Very true."

Socrates: "And of the names that attach to such things it would be fairest to attach the most beautiful to the most beautiful things?"

Protarchus: "Naturally."

Socrates: "And are not mind and wisdom the names we put first?"

Protarchus: "Yes."

Socrates: "Then these names would be rightly attached and accurately assigned to notions of reality as it really is."

Protarchus: "Certainly."

And if there was a pure form of knowledge, there must also be a well-understood prerequisite for the attainment of it. Socrates speaks again:

"If it is not possible while we are in the flesh to have pure knowledge of anything, there are only two alternatives, either knowledge is not possible at all or only possible when we are dead, for then the soul will be itself by itself and out of the flesh, but not before. So while we are alive we shall, it seems, be nearest to knowledge, if as far as possible we keep no company with the flesh and share nothing with it except what is absolutely necessary. We must not be infected with its nature, but keep ourselves pure from it, until God himself releases us. Pure like this and rid of the follies of the flesh ourselves, we are like to be with others of the same sort and shall come to know by experience all that is undefiled; and that is, I take it, the truth. For it is ordained that what is not pure shall not lay hold of what is pure."

Plato believed in the existence of a divine power and

in the guidance of this power. He believed in prayer, in the immortality of the soul, and in a future life. But still he felt that there might be something lacking. A speaker in one of the dialogues shows that Plato felt that there was still something beyond his reach:

> "About the immortality of the soul a man must adopt one of three courses. He must either be taught how the matter stands or find out for himself, or, if that is impossible, he must at least get the best account of the matter that human reason can provide and the most difficult to disprove. Mounted riskily upon that as upon a raft he must make the voyage of life, unless it may be possible to travel more safely and securely on the firmer foothold of some word of God."

Plato could never know what this missing element was, but to the Christian the answer was obvious. For Plato, the highest good was justice, or more properly, "righteousness."

> "I would now like to define for you without any frills just what *I* think righteousness and unrighteousness are. I call the reign of passion and fear and pleasure and grief and jealousies and desires in the soul emphatically unrighteousness, whether it does any damage or not. But the notion of the Best, in whatever way a city or any particular individuals think to secure it, I say is entirely righteous if it prevails in the soul and regulates the whole man, even if some loss is incurred. Action on these lines is righteous, and the part of a man that is subject to this control is righteous and the best thing in the whole of human life, even though many reckon the loss to be injustice of an unintentional kind."

Thus it was that the cities of the Christian Empire in the early years of the sixth century lived in a thought-world that had two origins: Greek and Judaeo-Christian. The intellectual adventure which had produced the Greek tradition was by itself an achievement that had put man on a different plane. It had shown the power of the human intellect and the possibilities of human reasoning. It had shown what could be accomplished by the human mind alone. It had shown the nature of the individual and the nature of the individual in the human community. Beyond this lay the unseen world of abstract truth, and the seen and the unseen made one whole which was governed by certain powers called "God" or "gods"; but here Plato could never be quite sure, and he was a theist, a monotheist, and polytheist, all at the same time. It was still in the realm of the individual and the community that the Greek thinkers had been most sure of themselves.

Nevertheless, it was a tremendous achievement, and every student in the schools of Gaza was indebted to it.

But what of revelation?

The result of revelation was not an achievement of the human mind; it was much greater than any such achievement could be. The incarnation of divinity in human life had changed the direction of human thought. Formerly, in the classical world, man's thought had been centered on man. Now, in the Christian world, man's thought was to be centered on God, for it had now become certain that man was significant only in relation to God. The whole of human intellectual activity received a new sanction and a new goal.

If the Incarnation manifested the true nature of man, the preparation for the Incarnation went much further back than the birth of Jesus, and the history of the Christian church began with the Book of Genesis. The truth was announced in the narrative of the Creation, which was likewise the opening chapter of the Christian Scriptures. The whole of the Scriptures was permeated with this initial proclamation of the truth, namely that God was the creator of all things and that He created man in His own image and likeness. Christian teaching was devoted to the working out of this theme and to the demonstration of its implications and its consequences.

The Old Testament as the record of the rule of God established in manifold fashion the truth that Elihu spoke to Job: "God is greater than man. Why dost thou strive against him?" God was acknowledged as maker of heaven and earth and of all things visible and invisible, and if man, given liberty, fell away from God and clouded the image of the divine within himself, Christ brought reconciliation and redemption. And Christ was still at work in the world, as Luke recognized when he spoke in the Book of Acts of his earlier gospel as "the treatise of all that Jesus began both to do and to teach."

Thus it was that man came to know that his salvation was to be achieved by his solidarity with Christ, that is, by his growing into the likeness to God (an idea that Plato had taught, in his own terms). As in Adam all died, so also in the Christ would all be made alive. And so, if any man comes to be "in Christ," there is a new creation

—a new creation within the man himself and a new outlook on creation for him.

Discerning in this way his divine sonship and realizing himself as joint heir with Christ, man came to understand that the Spirit of God is in man not only as life but also as wisdom and understanding. The pagan poet whom St. Paul quoted in his speech to the men of Athens on the Areopagus had written that men are the offspring of God; but how much more this meant to a Christian than to a pagan!

This was how a Christian could reach the answer to Pilate's question. (Was it a question that Pilate himself would have been able to understand?) Every Christian, at all times and in all places, came to the answer differently, but the answer was great enough to manifest itself to every man.

The question "What is truth?" implied the further question "What is the source of truth?" This, almost as much as anything else, had been at the bottom of the original conflict between paganism and Christianity when Christianity had emerged from its first conflict with Judaism and had moved out into the pagan world. True, there were times, as in the thought of Plato and the Stoic philosophers, when pagan ideas of truth almost seemed to touch Christianity, but on the question of the source they could not touch. For Greek philosophers and men of science, the source of truth was the human intellect, and the human mind was capable of dealing with any problem, intellectual or scientific, that it came upon.

The Christian knew that he had passed beyond this,

that he had passed from death into life, but his conception of truth as something dwelling in God and coming from God enabled him to see the pagan intellectual achievement in its true light. From an initial aversion to pagan philosophy as being only "vain deceit," Christian thinkers had come to see that Christian truth was large enough to subsume the pagan achievement and incorporate the best parts of it into Christian thought. Clement of Alexandria, Origen, and the three great Cappadocian Fathers, Basil the Great, Gregory of Nazianzen, and Gregory of Nyssa, had made it clear that the sovereignty of Christian thought was in no way threatened by pagan philosophy and pagan literature. On the contrary, the Christian tradition could be enriched by the best thought of the pagan writers. The Christian philosopher could embrace the whole of the human intellectual heritage.

The classical philosophers had believed that the way to truth was through knowledge and that knowledge, supplying a man with the truth, would give him virtue. But virtue, to the Christian, was more than it was for the pagan because to the Christian it was a gift of God.

And so Gaza, in the land of the Old Testament, had come to embody all of the traditions which had joined to constitute the thought world of that day. In a place such as Gaza, Hellenic, Judaic, and Christian threads could come together. When the citizen of Gaza took stock of the equipment of his mind, it became clear that if the achievement of the Greek thinkers was seen in the light of the Christian revelation, then the true magnitude of what had happened to man's intellect could be understood. The intellectual force and brilliance of Greece provided the basis upon which Christianity could form its message in terms which would be intelligible to the pagan world, trained in the Greek tradition. The citizen of Gaza, along with his fellows in all the other cities of the Empire, could perceive that it was for him and for them to enjoy the best of the word of man and of the Word of God. The words of the psalmist had taken the place of the words of Sophocles:

> When I consider thy heavens, even the work of thy fingers; the moon and the stars which thou hast ordained;
> What is man, that thou art mindful of him? and the son of man, that thou visitest him?
> Thou madest him lower than the angels, to crown him with glory and worship.
> Thou madest him to have dominion of the works of thy hands; and thou hast put all things in subjection under his feet:
> All sheep and oxen; yea, and the beasts of the field;
> The fowls of the air, and the fishes of the sea; and whatsoever walketh through the paths of the seas.
> O Lord our Governor, how excellent is thy Name in all the world!

VI.

Going to School

The Greeks seek after wisdom.
                              —I CORINTHIANS

IF THE INTELLECTUAL HERITAGE of a city of the Christian Empire in the early sixth century was a noble one, it was by no means a routine matter for a child in that world to obtain an education. In fact, it could not even be taken for granted that most people would be able to learn to read and write.

The Empire regarded education as a private, individual concern, and the state was not considered responsible for the literacy of its subjects. This view, which no one had ever thought to question, went back to the doctrine of Aristotle and the other classical Greek thinkers which colored so much of the life of the classical world, namely that men were not by nature created equal; that their natural endowments differed; that some were born to rule and others were born to serve; and that the latter were not fitted for education. The conditions of the servile life, it was believed, warped the mind and the spirit and made a man incapable of any kind of altruistic thought or intellectual endeavor. Hence only certain members of the community were eligible for education in the first place; moreover, it was the responsibility of the individual and his family to secure whatever education was open to him. Some monasteries educated orphans who had been entrusted to them, and cathedrals and large churches maintained schools for choir boys. There had from time to time been public endowments for the education of poor children, but these were the exception rather than the rule. The state felt no obligation in this direction, and if illiteracy had always existed alongside the ability to read and write, then illiteracy was a part of the natural order of things and was to be accepted by everybody, both literates and illiterates.

If the student had to shift for himself, the teacher also had to depend on his own resources. When the universities awarded no degrees and there was no public control of the qualifications of a teacher, anyone who wished to become a teacher might set up for himself and continue to teach as long as he could attract pupils. Inevitably there were all kinds of teachers offering instruction, individually and in privately owned schools, and a parent in search of a teacher for his child might find a wide range of fees which were demanded by different schools and instructors. A successful teacher might become wealthy, and such a man might accept promising but poor students at reduced fees or sometimes even remit fees altogether. A teacher of demonstrated ability or with friends in the right places—or both—might be appointed by a municipal government to its local public chair of rhetoric, in which he would receive a salary, plus private fees. A very fortunate teacher might be appointed to a chair in the imperial university in Constantinople, or he might become head of his own private school in one of the established centers of higher education: Athens, Constantinople, Alexandria, and Gaza.

But for such prosperous and distinguished luminaries, there were numbers of the less able, or the less fortunate, spending their lives in a narrow routine, sometimes in a dingy town, with unpromising pupils. The lives of such men were very hard indeed, and their experiences were reflected in their tempers. In an age when brutal physical punishment and torture were an accepted part of the legal system, school children had to expect harsh physical discipline, and flogging was frequent and severe. The teacher's life could not always seem attractive, yet the profession continued, as it always had, to attract aspirants.

The child, beginning its education in a system such as this, was dependent not only on its own ability and industry but also on the ability of its family to pay for good schooling—and then, of course, on the availability of a good teacher or school. Some households could afford private tutors, and these might be men of excellent quality, living in the house as members of the family, loved and respected, and able to form the character of the children as well as to give academic instruction.

Sometimes, again, some of the teaching—and on occasion a considerable part of it—could be given by a grandmother or an older sister. Indeed, it was quite often grandmothers and older sisters who taught small children to read and write, using the letters of the alphabet carved out of wood. Some farmers filled up their time during the bad weather in the winter carving the letters, sometimes out of fine hardwood which was then highly polished.

When it had learned its letters, a child would study literature, grammar, and arithmetic until it was twelve or fourteen. There was also physical training, including dancing, and music, and supervised games were considered important. There was a great deal of memorizing of passages from classical literature, for it was considered that a well-stocked mind prepared a man to be a ready speaker, able to adorn a public discourse or hold his own in an argument. Memorizing had always been regarded as the best way to acquire information and keep it at instant command; the person dependent upon written notes or books was liable to forget things that he should have available in his mind at all times.

When the child had thus learned to read easily and had been trained in the use of correct language, there began a second phase in which work centered on rhetoric and on its use in writing, declamation, and debate. The student had to compose essays, imaginary speeches, and dialogues of famous characters of history, along with formal descriptions of places and episodes. In all such composition the student was carefully trained to study the style and technique of the great masters of literature.

The aim of this training was not merely literary. A polished style was of course the sign of an intelligent and well-trained mind, and rhetoric was the basis of the art of persuasion. But more was involved. The great writers of the classic age, beginning with Homer, had devoted themselves to the study and delineation of human character, and the student who had been trained to analyze these pictures would himself benefit from their examples or their warnings. The emphasis on rhetoric and literary criticism might at first sight appear to be disproportionate, but these skills were thought of as providing the instruments for the more important study of humanity and the formation of moral character. In classical Greece, the proper study of mankind had been man, and man could best be understood from the writings of the great students of human nature, the poets, dramatists, philosophers, and historians. The training of young men along such lines was considered to be so successful that no other system was ever contemplated.

When the student reached the age of sixteen or seventeen, he might have to stop and go to work, or he might be able to go on to higher studies. Here he would continue his training in literature and rhetoric, now adding the study of philosophy and of mathematics, which was supposed to purify the mind and prepare it for the study of philosophy. Natural science was studied as a branch of philosophy, and in the speculative and theoretical rather than the practical aspect. Science was meant to be investigated for the sake of its relationship to man.

Man was the center of the universe, therefore one studied the universe, and nature, from the point of view of man and human life. An example will suffice. A distinguished mathematician and architect of Constantinople, in the reign of Justinian, conceived a device that was in effect a steam engine: a large metal vessel filled with water and covered with leather in which a leather tube was inserted. Heating the water produced steam pressure and vibration at the end of the tube. The idea was doubtless drawn from the writings of the Hellenistic scientist, Hero of Alexandria, who in the second century B.C. had described the principle of the use of steam. But the device in Constantinople was constructed in order to carry out an elaborate practical joke, and the highly educated gentleman of the imperial capital observed that it demonstrated the correctness of Aristotle's theory of the origin of earthquakes. It never seemed to occur to anyone in the sixth century, any more than to anyone in Hero of Alexandria's day, that a steam engine might have a practical use.

The young man who was able to go on for higher studies might find what he wanted at home, but for the best possible education he would have to go to one of the famous centers in which there had grown up communities of scholars that in later days would have been called universities. Each of these had its special academic atmosphere, different from the others. As always in the academic world, the atmosphere depended, to a large extent, on the personalities of the heads of the various schools. In all of classical education, the essential of the whole process was the personal relationship between teacher and pupil. The knowledge that was transmitted was handed on by the immediate association of one human being with another. This influence of the teacher on the student was not something extra, to be had if possible; it was indispensable. It was inseparably bound up with the quest for knowledge, a quest that the ancient Greeks had looked upon as almost sacred. Without it, knowledge and ideas would not be the same. The written word as preserved in a book could be put aside, lost, or misinterpreted, but the attentive student could never forget the spoken word of his master.

So the young man of Gaza, having to make a decision with regard to the place to go for his higher studies, often chose a certain city or a certain school because of the presence there of a particular teacher whose fame attracted him. Sometimes a young man might go from one city to another, seeking to hear several famous teachers in succession.

This was sometimes a difficult enough choice, but there was an even harder choice to be made, which was a choice between two poles. Athens had once been the single pole of education. Now there was a second pole: Jerusalem. The difference between these two poles symbolized, not merely a tension in educational theory, but a whole attitude toward life. In the Gaza of the early sixth century, this tension could be seen and understood perhaps more clearly than ever before.

VII.

The Christian Scholar

Then said he unto them, Therefore every scribe which is instructed with the kingdom of heaven, is like unto a man that is a householder, which bringeth forth out of his treasure things new and old.
—GOSPEL ACCORDING TO MATTHEW.

IF A YOUNG MAN OF GAZA wished to study law, he could go to one of the imperial law schools, at Constantinople and Berytus (Beirut), the only establishments at which the training of lawyers was permitted by the government. If the young man wished to pursue literary and rhetorical studies with a view to a career in the civil service, or as a teacher, or if he wished to study philosophy as the final step in a broad liberal education, there were several excellent possibilities at his disposal. The oldest "university town" of the Empire was Athens, still living in the glow of its ancient greatness, where there were schools which were the direct descendants of the celebrated academies of Plato, Aristotle, and the Hellenistic philosophers.

Alternatively, a young man might go to one of the more recent foundations: Constantinople, Gaza, or Alexandria. Each of these cities offered the same method of training in advanced studies in the humanities, but with different emphases and specialties for which they had become well known.

Constantinople was the center of a brilliant group of men of letters whose work was encouraged by the Emperor Justinian. There was also the imperial university, founded by Theodosius II in A.D. 426, with lecture rooms in the Capitol. There were ten professors of Latin grammar and philology and three professors of Latin literature and rhetoric. On the Greek side there were likewise ten professors of grammar and philology, but five professors of Greek literature and rhetoric. The capital naturally attracted young men who had a career in the civil service in mind.

Alexandria, older than Constantinople, had a somewhat different tradition. Famous in the Hellenistic period for the institute for advanced study founded by Ptolemy II, Alexandria had always had a special interest in mathematics and natural science, and while philosophers and men of letters had always been active there in teaching and research, Alexandria was the place to which a young man with scientific interests would go.

In intellectual and artistic matters, Gaza had traditionally looked to Alexandria. Academically, the Palestinian city was in a sense an outpost of the Egyptian metropolis. Many of the young men of Gaza, preparing for an academic career, had gone to Alexandria to complete their studies and then had returned to Gaza to launch their careers.

But there had come a time when the intellectual circles of Gaza had outstripped their alma mater. A succession of distinguished men of letters, beginning in the latter part of the fifth century, made Gaza the most prominent center of advanced literary study of its day.

One of the most prominent of these literary men, whose career is typical, was Procopius of Gaza (not to be confused with Procopius of Caesarea, who was probably one of the former's pupils). Procopius' dates are not known with certainty, but he was active in the reign of Anastasius (A.D. 491–518). He had studied at Alexandria, and in one of his letters he calls that city "the common mother of literary studies." Beginning his career as a teacher of rhetoric at an unusually early age, he made such a success that Berytus, Antioch, Tyre, and Caesarea, the capital of Palestine, all attempted to secure his services, but he always preferred to remain at Gaza.

It is recorded that Procopius wrote on a variety of subjects, both pagan and Christian. In the classical manner he composed a panegyric on the Emperor Anastasius (every man of letters was expected to produce such pieces) and a formal lament on an earthquake which had occurred at Antioch. One of his most remarkable pieces is a complicated and stylized description of a clock at Gaza, clocks being then a rarity set up only in public places. Another characteristic piece is a description of two paintings at Gaza depicting scenes from the story of Phaedra and Hippolytus of Euripides.

In all this Procopius was the successor of a long line of Greek writers who had devoted themselves to the study of Greek prose and poetry as an instrument of the highest literary art. But Procopius was at the same time a devout Christian. Along with his classical compositions he produced a series of theological writings. At that period, much of religious thought was embodied in commentaries on books of the Bible, and Procopius followed the custom of his time in writing an important commentary on Isaiah. His magnum opus in this line seems to have been a commentary on the Octateuch which a later literary historian characterizes as perhaps overly copious because Procopius took care to cite all the opinions of all the authorities. He also commented on the Books of Kings, Chronicles, and Proverbs and the Song of Solomon. Every theological writer in those days became engaged in polemics, and Procopius, like the others, used his commentaries to attack his theological opponents. He also composed a refutation of the philosophical doctrine of his older contemporary, the famous Neoplatonist Proclus.

Procopius was in his day the most distinguished man of letters in Gaza, and the honor passed to one of his pupils, Choricius, whose chief work was done in the 520's and 530's. Like his teacher, Choricius wrote in the classical style on both pagan and Christian subjects. The works which are best known today are the descriptions of the Churches of St. Sergius and St. Stephen at

Gaza, which pieces formed a part of two panegyrics Choricius composed in honor of his friend Bishop Marcianus, who had been his fellow student under Procopius. In the brilliancy of his rhetoric, Choricius was thought to have surpassed his master, and his work was commended by Photius of Constantinople, the scholar and critic of the ninth century:

> He [Choricius] is a lover of clearness and purity of style, and if he expatiates for any useful purpose, the clearness of his thoughts is no way impaired, since the expansion is not ill timed and never reaches the length of a complete period. In his writings, character and sincerity are combined, while at the same time he does not neglect the inculcation of moral lessons. As a rule he uses carefully selected words, although not always in their proper sense; for sometimes, owing to his unrestricted use of figurative language, he falls into frigidity, and sometimes is carried away into the poetical style. But he is at his best in descriptions and eulogies. He is an upholder of the true religion and respects the rites and holy places of the Christians. . . . Many writings by him of various kinds are in circulation; one meets with fictitious, laudatory, and controversial speeches, monodies, nuptial songs and many others.

Photius' only criticism of Choricius is that he introduced Greek myths and stories into his writings, even when dealing with sacred subjects. But such interpolations, frowned upon in Photius' time, had been regarded as elegant in Choricius' day. Choricius was fond of quoting the great classical masters, and the index of the modern edition of his surviving works shows that in 544 printed pages of Greek text he quotes Aeschines 29 times, Aristophanes 47 times, Demosthenes 142 times, Homer 274 times, and Libanius 493 times. It is characteristic of his epoch that he quotes Plato 356 times but Aristotle only twice.

Around the names of Procopius and Choricius are grouped those of a number of other savants and literary figures, who, if not so distinguished, are instructive for the interests and activities of the learned world of Gaza. One of these, John of Gaza, produced a hexameter account of a great painting in a public bath, an allegorical representation of the world and the powers of nature, which were represented personified in human form, such as Wisdom, Virtue, the Moon, the Four Winds, and Earth and her children—the Fruits, Europe, Asia, the Sea, Winter, and the Rains. The description of this vast and complicated picture opened with a Christian introduction, and in the middle of the poem the author describes a representation of the Cross, a feature which in the context seems so unusual that it has been suggested that this had been added in the Christian era to an originally pagan painting.

The list of the other authors of Gaza presents a varied catalogue of works. Zosimus of Gaza, a member of the generation preceding Procopius, was known for his commentaries on the classical orators Lysias and Demosthenes. At about the same time the rhetorician Aeneas of Gaza produced a curious work entitled *Theophrastus*, in which the philosopher of that name, the pupil and successor of Aristotle, is depicted being overcome by Christian arguments concerning immortality and the resurrection. That the author chose as his protagonist a personage who lived three centuries before the time of Christ was probably reckoned as a sign of originality. The work shows that the writer was familiar with the writings of Plato, Plotinus, and Gregory of Nyssa. Bishop Zacharias of Mitylene, who came from Gaza and who composed a well-known church history in Syriac (which was very likely his own native tongue), wrote a dialogue entitled *Ammonios* in imitation of Aeneas' *Theophrastus*. In a setting reminiscent of Plato's *Phaedrus*, a discussion takes place between a jurist and the Neoplatonist philosopher Ammonios concerning the problem of the eternity of the world.

One of the most characteristic figures of the era is that of Timothy of Gaza, who had been a pupil in Alexandria of the Egyptian scholar Horapollon. Timothy wrote both a treatise on animals and a work on syntax, illustrating the literary character of science and scholarship at this period.

Among the writers trained in the schools of Gaza, one of the best known was Procopius of Caesarea, who became the famous historian of Justinian's reign. Procopius' style shows that Thucydides must have been a favorite model in the classrooms at Gaza and that Herodotus must have been carefully read as well.

How is this sudden flowering of the schools of Gaza in the early sixth century to be accounted for? We know that Gaza had always had adequate instruction in literary and rhetorical studies, but what explains the sudden appearance of men of exceptional talents such as Procopius of Gaza and Choricius?

So much of the ancient literary evidence is lost that we cannot be sure of the answer. We would be justified, however, in supposing that the physical setting of the city had something to do with this excellence in belles-lettres. The whole atmosphere of Gaza was congenial to quiet literary study. Alexandria and Constantinople were able to attract and retain distinguished professors, but neither the one, as a busy commercial seaport, nor the other, as the imperial capital and the business center of the Empire, could match the attractions offered by Gaza to students and professors alike. The handsome classical buildings and the equable climate made Gaza an eminently pleasant residence for academic folk. The festivals and fairs, with their literary displays and contests, attracted visitors from all over the Graeco-Roman world, who served as appreciative audiences for the recitations of the professors and their pupils. Aside from the business life of the city, there was no distraction such as one would encounter at Alexandria or Constantinople. When a man of exceptional gifts emerged, such as Procopius of Gaza, the attractions of his native place led him to resist the enticements of other cities. These attractions doubtless also played a part in bringing students to Gaza.

But, one would think where there was any consideration of such factors as climate and physical setting, Athens would surely have exercised a stronger drawing power than Gaza, for the Palestinian city could never offer to the student the rich traditions and almost sacred associations that still clung to the name of Athens.

How is it, then, that when Gaza was enjoying the successes of Procopius and Choricius, Athens produced no figure of comparable stature? Indeed, the last distinguished name associated with Athens is that of the Neoplatonist Proclus, who died in the year 485.

The answer may be found in the situation which produced Justinian's famous action of the year 529. Having had the advantage of a preparatory period during which he was the chief assistant and adviser to his uncle, Justin I (A.D. 518–527), Justinian, when he came to the throne himself on his uncle's death, had some well-defined notions of what he wished to accomplish. One of the first problems to be taken up was the complete unification of faith and culture. This had long been a difficulty for Christian thinkers and for their sovereigns as well. Even after the conversion to Christianity of Constantine the Great, it was plain that the whole Empire was not going to be Christianized at once. Intellectual circles, where the classical tradition was well entrenched, were the longest to resist the gifts offered by Christianity, and while some Christian thinkers such as Origen and the Cappadocian Fathers had shown that Christianity was capable of absorbing the pagan tradition and transmuting it to its own ends, there continued to survive a body of pagan intellectuals who could not be reached by Christianity. If enough men clung to paganism, the Church could not look upon itself as wholly triumphant.

This situation, Justinian saw, was important for the future of education. It had been amply shown that the best literary education ought to take advantage of the great works of the classical masters. But unless these writings were taught, and studied, within the framework of Christian truth, there was no value in using them. They could in fact be dangerous if taught without reference to the Christian way of life.

Athens and Gaza illustrated Justinian's point exactly. Both were teaching classical rhetoric and philosophy and using the classical authors as literary models. But there was a difference, and this was of the utmost significance. The professors at Athens were pagans, while the professors at Gaza were Christians. At Athens the teachers were living in an ancient intellectual shrine, teaching the ancient authors, and teaching them in the old tradition. For these teachers, life might not seem to have changed since Hellenistic times. The teachers at Gaza represented a new type, the Christian scholar. They taught the classical authors because they believed in the value of this material; but they were themselves Christians, and in their instruction they essayed to show that the classical masterpieces had to be set within the larger framework of Christian truth and that if they were taken up from this point of view, they could make their appropriate contribution to Christian education. The sincerity of the outlook of the professors of Gaza was demonstrated by their writing on both classical and Christian subjects at the same time, and their appreciation of the value of the classics was measured by the success of their own classical writings.

Any sovereign intent upon the cultural and religious unification of his empire could have had no choice, and Justinian was amply justified in issuing his celebrated decree of A.D. 529. This edict (like some similar decrees of following eras) was not always understood properly by later generations, and it is quite possible that it was criticized at the time it was issued. Justinian did not intend to put an end to the teaching of classical philosophy at Athens. Certainly classical philosophy continued to be studied at Constantinople, Gaza, and Alexandria. What Justinian forbade was the teaching of classical philosophy by instructors who were not themselves Christians. This action was perfectly logical, for pagan professors, by their teaching of classical philosophy, might corrupt the minds of inexperienced and uncritical students, and this was a threat to the stability of the state.

Athens had indeed become an anachronism, no longer able to play its true part in the higher education of the new Christian Roman Empire. The Athens of the Neoplatonists was a ghost, and the surviving segment of the classical world was a prisoner of its own tradition. Constantinople, Gaza, and Alexandria, heirs of the old traditions, had become the instructors of the new age.

VIII.

The Dome of Heaven

*Remember, Lord, those who bring offerings and perform fair
works in thy holy churches.*
—Liturgy of St. John Chrysostom

CLEAR AIR AND BRIGHT SUN were the perfect setting
for the architecture of classical Greece, and every city of
the Mediterranean world beheld in its buildings the principles of taste worked out long ago on the shores of
the Aegean. The Romans, succeeding the Greeks, had
evolved their own expression in building, more massive,
more rich in decoration than the lighter Greek style. And
the lands to the east of the Empire had contributed a
taste for the interplay of sunlight and shadow on carved
architectural ornament. The customary type of building
that resulted as the familiar style of the Graeco-Roman
world was well adapted to the climate and to the needs of
the people whom the buildings were designed to serve.

Heir to all this tradition, Gaza in the early sixth century exhibited the architectural compositions and settings that had come to be part of the life of any such

city. Its colonnaded streets, public baths, administrative buildings, library, theater, and hippodrome recalled the classic Graeco-Roman forms.

But there was a new architectural factor in the world of the early sixth century: the Christian church. Just as the pagan city had been dominated by its temples to the old gods, the Christian city was dominated by its churches. In some cities, some of the old temples had been preserved as museums or had been converted into churches. In Gaza, however, the temples had been destroyed in the days of the celebrated Bishop Porphyry, and the churches had taken their place alongside the traditional public buildings.

The history of church architecture was the history of the Church itself. The early disciples had met "from house to house," breaking bread, praying, and teaching, as narrated in the Book of Acts. As the Church grew, some of the private houses in which the little groups had met were rebuilt and transformed into meeting places specifically adapted for worship and instruction.

From the beginning, the Church, when it was able to build publicly and on a larger scale, began to work out its own architectural style. At first it adopted the Roman basilica, the longitudinal three-aisled building with an apse at one end, designed by the Romans for judicial and commercial uses. This plan could be adapted to the needs of Christian worship, and it placed the public meetings of the Church in a dignified setting which carried the connotation of authority, both for Christians and for pagans who were still outside the Church.

The basilica plan always continued to be used, but as time passed the Christian clergy and Christian architects began to work out new plans which seemed to express more clearly the spirit of the Church's worship and were likewise more naturally adapted to the elaboration of the Church's ceremonial. All this was developing while the services of worship, especially the Divine Liturgy, or Holy Communion, were evolving into increasingly mature and authoritative forms, and the architects sought to supply settings which answered to the new expressions of the Church's worship and provided new opportunities for pictorial decoration, important both for the devotional life and the teaching ministry of the Church.

The new styles that came to be used, alongside the basilica, were partly developed out of the basilica itself, partly based on other concepts. An important step was made when two transverse arms were added to the apsidal end of the basilica, thus providing the symbolic ground plan of the cross. Domes were added, placed over the four arms and over their central crossing, providing symbols of the hemisphere of the heavens, which could be decorated with scenes of the life of Christ and of the apostles, prophets, and saints.

The architects worked out variations of the cross plan —sometimes the long form with an elongated nave, sometimes the square form with all arms of equal length. In some churches this latter form was enclosed within a square exterior.

Other major innovations were the octagonal plan and

the circular plan. The former was familiar in the proto-
type built by Constantine the Great at Antioch in Syria.
Both the octagonal and the circular forms gave a new
opportunity for elegance of decoration and for an effect
of lightness and unity in the interior which provided for
priests and worshipers a devotional setting that was at
once more spacious and more unified. Not the least of
the contributions of the new plan was the great dome
which now could cover and dominate the whole of the interior space, serving both as a magnificent setting for
the image of Christ and, through the windows at its base,
as a source of sunlight which pervaded the whole interior of the building.

The architects who conceived and planned these
churches were not the specialists in ecclesiastical architecture of later ages. Any architect would undertake to
design any building he was called upon to put up, though
some doubtless preferred churches to secular buildings.
Indeed, some architects, in the deeply religious world of
those days, would certainly have considered that the
greatest glory of their profession was the building of
churches. In addition to being less specialized than his
later successors, the architect also had a much wider and
a more individual background, and his training had been
along different academic lines. The architects who built
the churches of Gaza knew both more and less than their
colleagues of later epochs.

This was in keeping with the contemporary conception
of the sciences and the fine arts. In the classical understanding of the nature of human knowledge and its sig-

nificance for man, philosophy and theology were looked upon as the highest forms of intellectual activity. These studies of the mental and spiritual life of man and of the nature of the Divine Power were surely, it was thought, the most important subjects with which humanity could occupy itself. It was a natural consequence that science, and all other nonphilosophical and nontheological subjects, occupied a lower place in the intellectual world and in the general estimation of men. There were, to be sure, studies and occupations that were useful, such as architecture, medicine, mathematics, but these did not touch directly the highest reaches of human thought.

At the same time there was an ancient tradition, related to this one, which contributed greatly to its perpetuation. This was the tradition that a gentleman did nothing with his hands (warfare, athletics, and sport, as "gentlemanly activities," were an exception). The highest occupation for a gentleman was intellectual and philosophical inquiry. Indeed, it was believed that leisure and freedom from material cares were essential conditions for the best development of the powers of the mind.

If this excluded the working man from any possibility of the higher life of the mind, it created an ambiguity with respect to certain occupations which obviously involved both intellectual and manual activity. The physician, the architect, and the engineer all depended upon intellectual equipment and the use of the imagination, which of necessity involved a certain amount of practical activity as well.

A further variety of activity was to be found in the

work of artists—painters, sculptors, mosaicists, musicians. Perhaps silversmiths and goldsmiths might be considered worthy of mention here. Such people were more than artisans, but they could not quite be admitted to the same rank as the gentleman-intellectual or the intellectual, such as the physician, who engaged in practical activity.

It was obviously necessary to accommodate all these kinds of activities within the social structure. This was done by an extension of the principle of the distinction between the "theoretical" and the "practical." There was no question that there was a difference between, say, a philosopher as a "theoretical" man and a sculptor as a "practical" man. This principle was simply applied to the activities which seemed to partake of both natures, and it was considered that certain branches of knowledge were divided into theoretical and practical fields. For example, there was a theoretical aspect of medicine, and a gentleman could and should include this in his general program of education; but this kind of medical knowledge differed from the practical aspect of medicine, namely the treatment of the sick. This practical aspect had to be left to the practicing physician, for a gentleman could not engage in the actual practice of the medical art. In the area of what later came to be called "the fine arts," one could have an expert knowledge of painting, or of sculpture—that is, a "theoretical" knowledge—without engaging in the actual labor of painting or sculpting.

So it was with the science and craft of building. The men of the ancient world were much less conscious than their later brethren of "specialties" and of divisions between academic subjects. Mental compartments did not exist. Aristotle, for example, had been a biologist, and it would never have occurred to him to limit himself to botany, zoology, physiology, or anatomy. Similarly, the ancient builder was not specialized as an architect or a materials expert or a construction engineer. The builder had to be competent in everything relating to the activity of building. Indeed, the builder had to be trained in what later would have been called the science of mechanics. "Mechanics" was actually an over-all term employed by Pappus of Alexandria in his handbook of mathematics, a widely used compendium written early in the fourth century:

> The science of mechanics has many important uses in practical life, and is held by philosophers to be worthy of the highest esteem, and is zealously studied by mathematicians, because it takes almost first place in dealing with the nature of the material elements of the universe. For it deals generally with the stability and movement of bodies, and their motions in space . . . using theorems appropriate to the subject matter. . . . Mechanics can be divided into a theoretical and a manual part. The theoretical part is composed of geometry, arithmetic, astronomy and physics, the manual of work in metals, construction work, carpentering and the art of painting, and the manual execution of these things. The man who has been trained from his youth in the

aforesaid sciences as well as practised in the aforesaid arts, and in addition has a versatile mind, will be the best builder and inventor of mechanical devices.

This was a formidable training and doubtless not every aspiring builder or "mechanic" was able to master all the branches enumerated by Pappus. But the standard of knowledge and competence which was implied was a very high one, and the versatility of the aspirant was increased by the fact that after the regular academic preparation had been completed, the student put the finishing touches on his training by serving as an apprentice to an older practitioner. Here he had ample opportunity to observe the solution of the problems by an experienced mind. He could likewise witness the birth of new ideas and the inception of new methods and new styles. The active and intelligent apprentice could learn much more by associating with a mastermind than he could from all of his "theoretical" instruction.

Such was the training a young man of Gaza would expect to undergo if he hoped to become a "builder." The versatility of the most accomplished builder, and the type of mind he brought to bear on his architectural problems and ideas, can be illustrated from the careers of Anthemius and Isidorus, two of the most distinguished builders and engineers of the first part of the sixth century. They are known for their work in the construction of Justinian's great new Church of St. Sophia, The Holy Wisdom of God, in Constantinople, a feat that would have made the names of any architects immortal. But St. Sophia represented only a part of their accomplishment. They were employed by the Emperor Justinian for architectural and engineering projects throughout the Empire. What is most revealing about their conception of their calling is their activity in areas in which the architect of later epochs would not normally have expected to find himself. Isidorus was actually a professor of geometry or mechanics. He had revised the text of Archimedes, the greatest mathematician of antiquity, and he was cited as an expert on advanced problems of solid geometry in the two books (one of them written by one of his pupils) which were added as supplements to the thirteen books of Euclid. Isidorus wrote a commentary on the treatise *On Vaulting* of Heron of Alexandria, and in this Isidorus described a special compass he had invented for drawing parabolas.

Isidorus' colleague Anthemius was equally honored as a mathematician. He composed a treatise *On Burning-mirrors,* which is an important document in the history of conic sections. He also wrote a work *Concerning Remarkable Mechanical Devices,* which, unfortunately, has been lost. In Anthemius' writings we possess what seems to be the first mention of the construction of an ellipse by means of a string stretched tight about the foci. One of his colleagues, Eutocius, dedicated to Anthemius his commentaries on the *Conics* of Apollodorus.

To men such as Anthemius and Isidorus and to the men, whose names are lost, who built the churches of Gaza in the early sixth century, the designing and building of a new church was by no means a routine affair.

There were no handbooks, no photographs, no professional journals as there were in later ages. In order to see the work of other builders and of other times, a builder had to travel and examine buildings on the spot. There was much less standardization or uniformity of plans than there was in later ages and much less copying of existing monuments. Each new church was a new opportunity and a new challenge, and in the religious-minded society of that day the building of churches was the architectural field in which innovation and imagination found their greatest play. Other buildings, domestic and public, had arrived at a traditional style in which there was no longer much scope or incentive for new design and new decoration. It was the churches that called forth the builders' best efforts. Even if a new church was in general modeled on another, it was by its nature a unique building with its own individual characteristics.

The churches of Gaza have perished, but literature, "more enduring than bronze," has preserved accounts which bring to life the churches in which the people of Gaza worshiped in the early years of the sixth century.

One of these was the church of St. Sergius, founded by a governor of Palestine, Stephen, with the assistance of Marcianus, bishop of Gaza. St. Sergius was a famous early martyr of Mesopotamia—a witness to the Faith in the persecution under the Emperor Diocletian—to whom many churches throughout the Empire were dedicated.

The church in Gaza was cruciform in plan, with a dome over the intersection of the arms of the cross. Choricius, the famous professor, included a description of the church in a panegyric addressed to the bishop:

Make your way to the northern part of the city, pass through the market place, and turn to the left. Take your stand in the colonnade of the market place which lies outside the porch of the church. You will be undecided whether to satiate yourself with the view of the entrance, or to make your way immediately to the pleasures the interior seems to promise.

Above the colonnade running round the market place rise four columns of marble from Carystus in Euboea, conspicuous for their size and their wonderful colorings. The two in the center carry a stone arch decorated with a pattern of rings carved in high relief. The keystone carries the Cross, the symbol of the Savior's Passion, formed by the rings as they join together. The roof of the entrance is composed of four arches, forming a square plan, with a half-dome on either side over the wings of the colonnade.

Going up the steps, you pass into an atrium with four equal sides, each formed by a covered portico, carefully designed to be in the proper proportion with the open area. The capitals of the columns are joined by wooden beams, save at the two entrances, where the beams are omitted because at these points the columns carry arches. Each portico at its center has a semicircular niche; and being open to the breezes, the court is always a pleasant spot. In one of the porticoes is the place in which it is customary for the bishop to hold his official receptions. As you turn toward the entrance of the church itself, the breeze passes softly beneath your clothing and refreshes your body.

As you enter the church at its western end, the variety of the beauties you behold will cause you to stagger. Fear-

127

ing to leave something unnoticed, you will not let your gaze rest on anything.

Toward the north is the baptistry, surrounded by columns, designed for initiation into the Christian life. Its floor is embellished with variegated mosaics.

You now see the two side aisles of the church, one on the north, one on the south. The outer walls are faced with marble slabs, carefully cut and fitted so that the natural veins form ornamental patterns, rivaling the works of painters.

In the center of the church there are pillars supporting eight arches, symmetrically facing one another. In the east wall, toward the rising of the sun, stands the apse, a shell-like recess, semicylindrical, in which the bishop has his seat during services. On the two sides are smaller apses, similar in design.

In the hemisphere which crowns the central apse is placed a mosaic with gold and silver background, showing the Mother of the Savior laying the child, just born, on her bosom. Figures of pious men are shown on either side of the scene. At the right is that man, a ruler in every respect, who is worthy to be numbered among the saints and to bear the name of the chief of the deacons who served God, more especially because, with the bishop to share his labors, he presented the city with this shrine, knowing that a gift of a building would bring the city dignity, while the building of a church brings it not only beauty but godliness. We see him graciously requesting the patron saint of the church, St. Sergius, to accept the gift; and with gentle gaze the saint accepts the offering, and placing his hand on the governor's shoulder, he is about to set him beside the Virgin and her Son the Savior.

128

In the two smaller apses at the sides we see mosaics showing trees and vines in which one can almost feel the breeze blowing through the branches. The artist has also shown a pitcher of cool water, matching the coolness of the interior of the church. Beside this he has shown a flock of birds and partridges.

On the pendentives below the central dome are similar decorations of mosaic, showing pear trees, pomegranates and apple trees with bright fruit. In the pictures, these blossom at all seasons and need no water. Eagles with spreading wings perch on the trees or fly aloft.

As the eye rises to the roof of the church, it sees how the central pillars support a square which in turn carries an octagon above it; and on this the hemispherical dome itself rests. Here the decoration is all in gold, the eagles are set against a gold background, and gold blossoms about the arches, mixed in some places with blue, each color setting off the other.

Through the rhetoric of Choricius' description (here abbreviated and in part paraphrased) there can be felt very plainly the quiet, the lightness and the cool airiness, and the sense of spaciousness that were so characteristic of Greek churches. Pervasive throughout the building was the gentle fragrance of incense, which became part of the quiet and repose of the interior.

The mosaics, along with the church itself, have long since perished, but we can gain some notion of their style and beauty from the preserved mosaics in the "Dome of the Rock," the Mosque of Omar in Jerusalem, which were made about a century later than those in Gaza.

Choricius goes on to describe the altar, the "holy table," which was made of solid silver, with legs of silver. Kept highly polished at all times, this altar added its special color to the rich background of marbles, mosaics, and gilding. "Wealth [Choricius writes] that flows out for holy uses becomes an ever flowing stream for him who possesses it."

The walls, arches, and dome were all enriched with mosaics which served not only to beautify the church but to teach the stories of the Old and New Testaments to the folk of the congregation, many of whom either were illiterate or, if they could read at all, could read only slowly and very likely did not own a Bible.

The church contained so many pictures that Choricius did not feel it possible to describe all of them in his encomium of the bishop. He therefore omitted those on the lower walls and proceeded to lead the spectator's eye to the roof. Choricius' dramatic descriptions make the mosaics live once more in the mind's eye.

Here Choricius begins with the well-loved scene of the Annunciation, established in church decoration as the traditional opening of the cycle of pictures of the life of Christ. "Here is a winged being [Choricius writes], just come down from heaven, in the artist's fancy. He approaches the Virgin Mother, not yet a mother, and finds her engaged in spinning, a task suited to her dignity. He greets her with the good tidings. The maid, startled by the strange sight, has turned about quickly, and in fear she has almost dropped the purple stuff from her hand. Her innocence fills her with alarm, and her impulse is to doubt the angel's greeting."

"In the next painting [Choricius goes on] we see an ass, a cow, a manger, a child, and a maiden asleep, her left hand under her elbow and her cheek resting upon her right. She has brought forth a child, without the need of a union with man. Her face does not show the pallor of one who has just given birth for the first time; being chosen for miraculous motherhood, she was spared its natural pains."

The shepherds in the field are next described. "A cry from Heaven has caused them to leave their sheep who are grazing in the field and about the spring. They have set the dog to guard the flock, and they stand gazing up to heaven, each in an easy pose. Most of them have put aside their crooks, but one man is supporting his left hand on his crook, with his right arm raised in a gesture of wonder. An angel has come to meet them and is showing them the direction in which the child is to be found. The animals, silly creatures, pay no attention to the sight, but bury their noses in the grass or drink from the spring. But the dog, not welcoming strangers, gazes intently at the unaccustomed vision. The star which guides the shepherds is reflected faintly in the spring, whose waters are stirred up by the sheep."

The next scene showed the aged priest Simeon, rejoicing as the mother brings the child to the temple. Then the spectator would behold the marriage feast at Cana. The Savior was shown transforming the water into wine.

One of the servants takes a pitcher of water and fills the storage jars, while another fills the drinking bowls and goes around to the guests in turn, starting at the proper place. The wine seems to be of a very fine flavor, as one may see from the flushed cheeks of a man who has just drunk some of it. "All this [Choricius concludes] is an example of the Savior's love for mankind."

Other miracles were shown in turn, the healing of Peter's mother-in-law, the curing of the man with a withered hand, the saving of the centurion's servant. The raising of the son of the widow of Nain is described in some detail. "The young man is being carried out to the tomb, and the wailing women are with him. Crowded together, they partially hide each other, but as you look at them you feel that if they were separated, each one would be shown with her whole figure. Perhaps before the miracle they were standing separately, but as the Savior brought the boy to life, they ran to look, and came together."

The following scene shows the woman who was a sinner anointing the Lord's feet. Choricius speaks of her soft clothing and her golden ornaments.

Other scenes depicted Jesus walking on the water and saving Peter, the healing of the demoniac, the woman with an issue of blood, and the raising of Lazarus ("the women do not bear their joy quietly; for women are wont to cry out very easily in the presence of the unexpected").

Finally the artist painted the Passion and Glorification of Christ, ending with the Ascension. Thus, Choricius concludes, were fulfilled the predictions of the prophets who (according to the traditional iconography) are depicted near the dome.

Another church preserved for us by Choricius' pen was the Basilica of St. Stephen, which was outside the city. This was a three-aisled basilica, with galleries above the side aisles. Choricius, we see, chose for description two different types of churches. That of St. Sergius stood on the edge of the market place, one of the busiest spots in the crowded life of the city. In the Church of St. Stephen, Choricius shows us another characteristic type of Greek church, built in the open country, well beyond the city walls, and standing in its own quiet enclosure, surrounded by trees and gardens. Such a spot was devoted to peace and contemplation.

To reach the church, Choricius conducts his reader to the eastern gate of the city, opening on the road to Beersheba and the East. The city being built on rising ground, the road descended after it left the gate. The church was plainly in sight in the distance, and the promenade was rendered more agreeable by the covered stone colonnade that had been built along the road from the city to the church, providing shelter from the burning sun in the summer and from the rain in the winter.

As he drew nearer to the church, the visitor could examine it at leisure, for it was built on an eminence. At the side of the road, the monumental gateway to the church admitted the visitor to a flight of marble steps leading up to a handsome colonnaded porch and a square atrium formed by four richly designed porticoes. Here the visitor would pause to enjoy the breeze which made the shady porticoes a place of refreshment.

The church, square and solidly built and lacking all ornamentation on the exterior, rose on the eastern side of the atrium, its entrance flanked by two towers resembling watchtowers. The columns of the atrium were remarkable as being all from the same quarry and all of the same gleaming white color. On the side toward the church the columns were twice as tall as those on the other three sides—to add dignity to the entrance to the building. In the summer, the porticoes of the atrium served chiefly for the refreshment of visitors, but in the winter, at one of the annual festivals of St. Stephen, celebrated on December 26, they served to bring the worshipers into the church dry shod if rain happened to be falling. The martyr's other annual festival fell on August 2.

The portico on the right led to the dwelling of the priests and other servers attached to the church. From the opposite portico opened the garden designed for the bishop's public receptions, a spot made pleasant by the breezes and the vines and flowers with which it had been planted, as well as by the fountain of pure water which kept the garden cool and fresh. Here, Choricius writes, the bishop, speaking "with a voice sweeter than Nestor's," stood with a pure heart and smiling face, welcoming those who came to see him.

The eastern colonnade, on the side toward the church, was paved with the mosaics so popular at this time, showing the creatures and the foods produced by both the sea and by the land. Fruits, grains, vegetables, birds, fish, and shellfish—all were portrayed in decorative patterns which illustrated the bounty provided for man by God. The mosaicists, with their consummate skill, were able to depict each plant, each bird, and each fish with the most accurate detail and the most lifelike air. In a city such as Gaza, seafood formed one of the principal elements in the diet, and the spectator would appreciate and admire the artists' skill in depicting the creatures that traveled the paths of the seas.

Entering the church, the visitor would at once notice the union of harmony and taste which had governed its plan and construction. The proportions of nave and side aisles and their harmony with the height of the roof made the size of the whole interior seem perfect. This elegance of design was matched by the splendor of the marble revetments, of many colors, which the trained eye could see came from all the famous marble-bearing regions. These lent color and richness to the whole building.

All through Choricius' description we can feel the lightness and airiness of the church. The side aisles were two storied, the upper story, on both sides, being reserved for women, who, according to custom, were not permitted to mingle with the men during the services. The windows along the aisles admitted sunlight and breezes into the church in generous quantity.

The walls of the side aisles were decorated with scenes of the Nile, a favorite subject for ornamentation of both churches and private houses. This theme had originated in the realistic school of Hellenistic painting, and it remained a favorite with artists because of the variety of scenes and of treatment that the subject offered. In the church at Gaza, Choricius writes, the river itself was not shown, but its presence was indicated by means of its symbolic attributes and by scenes of the meadows along its banks, filled with all the various birds that were accustomed to live in the meadows and bathe in the stream. Here once more the mosaic artists could find full scope for their skill in the treatment of nature.

At the eastern end, before the sanctuary, stood four porphyry columns of the rich purple hue which was reserved for the emperor's clothing. The sanctuary was terminated by a semicircular apse which rose into a semidome. In the semidome was placed a mosaic showing the donor of the church, on the right, bearing in his hands a model of the building, with St. John the Forerunner on the left.

Choricius devotes all his skill to the description of the marblework in the apse:

> The lower part of the wall gleams with marbles of all kinds. Among these, one particular stone, cut into many forms, surrounds the window, which is both broad and tall in proportion, which lies in the middle of the lower part of the wall. This stone alone supplies the facings on either side along the edges of the window which it entirely surrounds, and, adorning the two walls on either side, it does not stop until it has mounted up on both sides and has reached the girdle resting on the window, which is itself of the same stone. In this way bands of marbles conceal the wall in well-joined fashion, and are so well fitted that you

would suppose them to be the work of nature; and they are so variegated by their natural colors that they do not fall short of human painting. Indeed, if the painters' students, whose task it is to choose and copy the fairest things in existence, should be in need of columns to reproduce, or lovely stones—and I have seen many such things painted —they will find many fine models here.

The literary climax of Choricius' description is the account of the wooden dome, which he describes in terms of a truncated cone. This rose at the eastern end of the church, over the apse, in the manner of the Church of the Nativity at Bethlehem. Here Choricius uses all his literary art, as well as his knowledge of geometry, to produce a tour de force that must have brought great admiration from his audience:

On one of the girdles of the apse—the highest one, I mean —there rests a novel shape. Geometrical terminology, I understand, calls this a half-cone, the term receiving its origin as follows: You have perhaps seen in your country the pine tree, and if this was originally a maiden—for there are some who tell this story, how Boreas, smitten with amorous jealousy, was about to slay her, when Earth, deeply pitying her plight, set up a tree of the same name as the maiden. I neither believe the people who tell this nor is it my intention to relate it, but only to say that it bears a fruit which is called the cone. This is the origin of the term applied to the form. This much I can describe to you by a graphic image. But if you wish to hear a full description, it is like this. A carpenter, cutting circles, or ribs of the framework, five in number, from the material of his craft,

wood, and cutting each of them equally in two, and joining
nine of these slices [or sectors of circles] to each other by
their tips, and also joining them by their middles [i.e., the
place where they had been cut equally in two] to the girdle
which, as I just now said, was the highest course of the
church, sets upon them panels of wood, which he hollows out
to the required pine-cone shape, equal in number to the
ribs, which begin in broad fashion from below and gradually become narrower and rise up to a sharp point, so as to
fit the concavity to the wall; and drawing together all the
tips into one, and bending them gently in a gradual curve,
he produced a most pleasing spectacle. But while I have
cut five circles in half I have described the function of only
nine of the sectors, and I realize that you are probably seeking the remaining part of the circle. This part, then, is
itself divided equally into two quarter sections, and one
part of it being placed on one side of the nine [i.e., of the
dome], and the other part on the other side, an apsidal
vault of the same material, wood, is formed on both sides,
each hollowed out in front, contributing to the beauty of the
image which is depicted there, in the middle, of the Ruler
of all things. And gold and colors make the whole work
brilliant.

Here Choricius is so intent on his geometrical display
that he does not describe in detail the mosaic of Christ,
the Pantokrator, the "Ruler of all things," which filled
the dome and formed the focus and the climax of the
decoration of the church. This image, as the center of
the decoration of every Greek church, showed Christ
with His gaze fixed upon the worshipers below. The eyes
seemed to meet the eyes of everyone who looked up at

the image. It was, indeed, impossible to escape this gaze. The figure was designed so that it seemed tremendous in size, filling the whole dome. The beholder was reminded of the words of the psalmist:

> The Lord is in his holy temple; the Lord's seat is in heaven.
> His eyes consider the poor, and his eyelids try the children of men.

. . .

> Behold, the eye of the Lord is upon them that fear him, and upon them that put their trust in his mercy.

Both to the worshiper during a service and to the solitary visitor, Christ was an ever present reality, caring for men, and everyone who beheld the great figure in the dome was reminded that he was living in the sight of the Lord. So it was in every church of the Greek world.

The promenade from Gaza to the solitary church beside the dusty road, surrounded by its tall, dark cypress trees, was like an excursion into the other world which the Church represented. For Choricius and his friends, the visit to the empty, silent church brought rest and beauty, contemplation and refreshment. In such a church time could be left behind, and the visitor could be aware that it was the invisible which was the real.

IX

Stewards of the Mysteries

Lord, I have loved the habitation of thy house,
and the place where thine honor dwelleth.
—PSALM XXVI

To THE CHRISTIAN, the church building was the center of worship, the visible dwelling of God and the gathering place of the Christian community for instruction, prayer, and praise. The church was indispensable for the life of the Christian community, and the Christian thought that he understood what the church meant for his personal religious life.

But did the Christian of Gaza in the early years of the sixth century really understand all that the churches in the city meant for him? By this time there were no pagan temples left in the city and no public pagan ceremonies and worship. Was it possible to understand all that Christianity meant if one did not appreciate what it was that Christianity had replaced?

There had been, to begin with, many types of pagan

cults and mystery religions and many varieties of philosophies which for some pagans had served in place of a
religion. To the Olympian gods and goddesses of Homer
and the early Greeks there had been added the Oriental
deities, who sometimes corresponded to Greek gods and
were identified with them or retained their native names
and cults. Mithras, Astarte, Isis, Baal, and Marnas
could, especially in Palestine, live side by side with Zeus,
Aphrodite, Apollo, Poseidon, and the other figures of
classical Greece. In a pagan city, before the days of
Christianity, a worshiper could go from temple to temple, seeking satisfaction for his religious aspirations and
hoping to obtain something from one god or another in
return for something done or offered to the god; or the
worshiper might merely perform a ceremonial duty of
formal worship which it was considered wise to keep up.
Prayer, burning of incense, sacrifice of offerings of food,
dedication of votive offerings, processions, festivals,
mystic initiations, ritual sleeping in temples, in some in-
stances ritual prostitution at the temples—the pagan
cults and the pagan philosophies had offered many things
to many men. A man could abandon a cult and become a
devotee of another, or give up one philosophical system
for another, as he wished. He could get whatever he could
from his religion. The detached observer would have no-
ticed that no one of these cults or systems of philosophy
had ever succeeded in imposing itself on the majority of
people or in supplanting the other cults and systems.

Here, of course, lay one of the secrets of the triumph
of Christianity. Christianity offered what the pagan

cults could not, and as a rule people recognized this when they came to understand Christianity properly. The pagan cults were on a different basis; and like the cults themselves, the temples did not possess the same religious significance. The Hellenistic kings and the Roman emperors had attempted, by means of the national cult of the deified ruler, to provide a single religious focus for their people, but at best this could be only an outward ceremony. The temple of the deified emperor and the temple of the goddess Roma could occupy a place of honor among other shrines, but they could hardly be expected to answer all of men's religious needs. Yet it was a good thing to provide for the orderly observance of the public rites. Plato had voiced the feeling of intellectuals and statesmen when in a passage in the *Republic* he wrote of the traditional cults in terms of "the founding of temples and sacrifices and the other cults of gods and demigods and heroes; and then the burial of the dead and the services it is necessary to perform for those in the other world in order to secure their favor."

All such cults were inevitably subject to abuses. Priests were sometimes venal and immoral. There were temples equipped with secret mechanisms for the performance of "miracles" during the rites. Among the simple peasants there was the grossest superstition, and spring rites, intended to insure the fertility of crops and herds, became the happy occasion for sexual "rites" among the country folk.

But as Plato wrote, man is the most god fearing of all living creatures, and there was another end of the scale:

among the religious souls who had come to a conviction
of the existence and the working of a single divine
power that ruled the universe. This faith was expressed
in different ways, for each man had to come to it himself. One could call the power Mind, or the Divine,
or "God," or whatever other name seemed appropriate.
One of the most famous manifestations of such belief
was the *Hymn to Zeus* of Cleanthes, a philosopher of the
third century before Christ:

Most glorious of the immortal gods, called by many names,
Almighty Zeus, author of Nature, ruling all with law,
Hail! Thee it is right that all mortals should address,
For we are thy offspring, and alone have received thy image
Among all things that live and creep upon the earth.
Therefore I hymn thee, and ever shall sing thy power.
Thee this universe obeys, whirling about the earth;
And wherever thou leadest it, it gladly is controlled by
    thy hand,
So strong a minister dost thou hold in thine unconquer-
    able hands,
The thunderbolt of heaven, flaming, with double edge . . . .
Thou dost direct the universal reason
Which moves through all things
And mingles with the greater and the lesser lights of
    heaven.
How great thou art, ruler most high among all!
No work comes to pass on earth without thee, O God,
Neither in the divine sphere of heaven nor on the sea,
Save for what is done by evil men in their folly.
But thou knowest both how to set the crooked straight

And make fair unlovely things; and unloved things for
    thee are loved.
For you have thus joined all good things with evil into one
So as to become, from all, one reason that is forever.
Which evil mortals still flee,
Men who ever desire the possession of material goods
Look not to the universal law of God, nor hear his voice,
Which if they obeyed with intelligence they would lay
    hold on the good life.
But now, unreasoning, one man seeks one thing, another
    something else,
Some in the unholy strife for fame,
Others in no decent fashion intent upon gain,
While others hasten to indulgence and the sweet pleasures
    of the body—
All of them finding that they gain the opposite of what
    they wished.
O Zeus, giver of good gifts, wrapped in black clouds, source
    of the lightning,
Deliver men from their wretched ignorance!
Scatter it from the soul, and grant that it find the wisdom,
Relying on which with justice thou dost govern all.
That, being honored, we may render thee honor in return,
Singing continually the praises of thy deeds,
For mortals should, since there is no greater honor, either
    for men or for gods
Than always to hymn in justice thy universal law.

Within the terms of Greek religious experience and of
Greek habits of visualization and expression, this noble
concept of the nature of Zeus found its visible realization in the temple and the cult statue—the temple being

indeed primarily the setting for the cult statue. The classic achievement in the visible representation of Zeus was the colossal gold and ivory statue by the celebrated sculptor Phidias in the Temple of Zeus at Olympia. Pausanias the traveler described the impression it made on the spectator:

> The god sits upon a throne; he is made of gold and ivory. On his head rests a garland which is made to resemble olive shoots. In his right hand he bears a Victory, which, like the statue, is of ivory and gold; she wears a ribbon, and, on her head, a garland. In the left hand of the god is a sceptre, ornamented with every kind of metal; the bird sitting on the sceptre is the eagle. The sandals also are of gold, as is likewise his robe. On the robe are embroidered figures of animals and the flowers of the lily. The throne is adorned with gold and jewels, and with ebony and ivory as well. . . . The height and breadth of the Olympic Zeus have been measured, but even these records fall far short of the impression made by the sight of the image. . . .

The figure was in fact forty feet high and was mounted on a base twelve feet high, so that the head of the statue almost touched the roof of the temple. The spectator, as he beheld it, would be overcome by the feeling that no earthly dwelling was able to contain such a divinity.

Cleanthes' hymn and Phidias' statue showed what a god and his temple could mean to the religious-minded Greek. But the pagan worshiper could never forget that around the figure of Zeus—as around all the other gods —there clustered a well-known collection of legends con-

145

cerning the private life of the father of the gods and his family. These episodes were detailed in very human terms, including examples of the majestic deity's weakness for feminine charms and his remarkable ingenuity in transforming himself into novel disguises which enabled him to visit earthbound ladies and take them by surprise. St. Augustine in *The City of God* quoted the famous saying of the distinguished Roman statesman Q. Mucius Scaevola that there were three classes of divinities: those handed down to us by the poets, those handed down by the philosophers, and those handed down by the statesmen.

Thus while the pagan temple had been a symbol, the dwelling place of a god and the result of human effort to realize, in monumental form, the majesty and the power of the god, the temple remained essentially a monument and a symbol. Its meaning could be determined only by the worship offered in it—and this worship could take place on all levels, from Cleanthes' salutation of the supreme deity to the orgiastic sessions of the Oriental cults. The temple, as a temple, could never be greater than the worship; and both temple and worship were man made. As religious expressions, they could go as far as man, in his independent, unaided religious thought, could go, but they could go no further. Men could devote their finest talents to the building of temples, the carving of statues, and the writing of music and hymns, but all this was only devised by man and only represented what man thought of the gods.

A church, considered simply as a religious shrine, existed on a different basis. It was, like a temple, a place of worship, the dwelling place of a deity, the gathering place of the faithful. Temple and church, each in its own way, served as centers for religious life. But there was an enormous difference. In a church it was a different kind of deity, revealed to men in different fashion and worshiped by men who stood in a different relation to the deity. Many times the pagan offered his worship so that the deity would grant something in return—a *quid pro quo*. Christian worship was the coming together of God and His people on terms that had never been possible in paganism, even in its highest forms.

This was because a church represented the belief, continuing from generation to generation and renewed in every generation, in the existence of a loving God, creator of all things visible and invisible, who had been incarnate on earth and had come among men as savior and redeemer. Nothing that paganism offered could match the incarnation and the saving and redeeming life of Christ. Nothing in paganism could match the Old and New Testaments. Indeed, no pagan religion was a religion of a book, as Judaism and Christianity were. The Olympian Zeus might be, in Homer's well-known phrase, "father of gods and men," but even great Zeus had not come to men in the self-revelation of the God who was creator of all mankind. Zeus was not the creator of either gods or men, and the Olympic hierarchy all came into being following the original act of creation. Zeus was a *pater familias* of an unruly family which he could not always keep under control. He was far from being a

147

loving father to whom his children could have immediate access in prayer.

Here lay the "open secret," the "mystery," embodied in the churches of Gaza. If the Christian Way had survived and grown for five hundred years of Christian history, it meant that every new generation had felt itself turned, literally "converted," toward God. And so every generation had found in its churches—whether it used old ones or built new ones—a continuing life of the tradition which was shown forth in the Scriptures and in the apostolic succession of the priesthood.

A church, then, stood both as a house of God and as a material embodiment of a tradition and belief. In its traditional scheme of pictorial decoration it preserved in visual form the memory of the Savior and of the cloud of witnesses. But it was not a monument detached from its people; it was not just an architectural masterpiece. Church and people came together in two ways, each distinct and unique.

First, the people who worshiped in the church had been taught that they themselves could let themselves "be built, as living stones, into a spiritual temple," a temple of which Christ Himself was the cornerstone. Christ was the only true foundation upon which the Christian could build. A church, then, was a symbol of the cohesion, the unity, and the strength of the people of Christ. The individual Christian was in fact a temple of the living God and of the Holy Ghost, to whom a church could serve as an exemplar of his own status.

But there was another way as well that brought the

believer and the building into a unique association. This was the traditional worship of the Universal Church, which had come to find its highest and most significant expression in the Eucharist, or Holy Communion, known in Greek-speaking lands as the Divine Liturgy.

Beginning, at the command of Christ, as a commemoration of the Last Supper ("Do this in remembrance of me"), the Liturgy had become, inevitably, the service in which Christ and His faithful met, Christ sacrificing Himself and the faithful sharing in that offering and sacrifice and thus realizing their true nature.

From its beginning as a re-enactment of the Last Supper, the Liturgy had been elaborated on the basis of growing Christian experience and deepening insight into its spiritual meaning. By the beginning of the sixth century it had reached essentially the form it was to have throughout the history of the Greek Christian East down through the Byzantine era. In this form, the Liturgy was not merely the rehearsal of the Last Supper and the repetition of the act of communion, but a reverent review of the birth, life, and work of Christ and of His death and resurrection. For it was all of these things that gave meaning to the act of communion, and it was by his repeated recalling of this life that the worshiper came to understand the act of communion and its meaning for himself.

More than this, the worshiper also could understand his own meaning for God and for the community of his fellows. For the communion was not a solitary act, bringing something to the single lone individual. It was an action at once individual and corporate in which the worshipers, receiving the bread and wine as the Body and Blood of the Savior, were made one with Him and with one another in the mystical Body of Christ, which was the blessed company of all faithful people. Here the communicant, as he looked about him at the throng standing with him, would see one more manifestation of the universal character of the Liturgy. For the service was the same for rich and poor, for those who were powerful in this world and for the humble. To the Eucharist came everyone in Gaza, from the wealthiest man in the city to the washerwoman, from the imperial governor to the itinerant fruit vendor, from the distinguished professors Choricius and Procopius to the illiterate fisherman. All these, as they stood together in the church—men and women separately, children and old people, the bishop, the priests, deacons, acolytes, singers, doorkeepers—all were children of God with access to the same Body and Blood. The worshipers knew that the richness of the building, with its eucharistic vessels of precious metals and the bishops and priests in elaborate and costly vestments, did not seem out of keeping with the known poverty of many of the congregation. This was the royal house into which the King of Glory came. The widows who could offer only a tiny coin should not be envious or discontented, for they knew that God was as close to them as He was to the rich—if not, sometimes, closer. The wealthy families of the city who gave much of the money for these churches and their adornment knew very well about the poor and knew that the poor would not resent the money being given for the building of churches instead of to them. This was expected of the wealthy; and before the shining silver altar of the Church of St. Sergius in Gaza—and before every altar throughout the Empire—all were equal.

Then, as his gaze traveled from his fellows to the walls, arches, and domes, the worshiper was reminded, by the silent pictures all about him, that his union was not only with his own contemporaries, his neighbors, whom he could see. The Liturgy, in its words and teaching, looked forward and backward at the same time—backward to the action of God in history, to the earthly ministry of Christ, and to the witness of the Church in its history, forward to the growth and perfecting of the Body of Christ. Thus the communicant, as he partook of the mystery and received the Body and Blood which were steadfastly offered to him, felt himself at one with the whole of the cloud of witnesses, both those who had gone before him and those who would come after him. The Liturgy served to unite the two worlds, the visible present world and the unseen world which was the true one.

As the setting for this union and this realization, the church building stood as the unique and indispensable physical framework. The church was not merely a beautiful architectural composition or a place to be visited in holy days. It was the place to which a Christian could come to realize his true self, to receive strength with which he could go out to his work in the world. In the mundane world it was still possible to dwell in the House of the Lord forever.

There was yet another way in which, to a Christian familiar with the tradition of classical cults, a church differed from a temple. This was in one of the most important adjuncts to worship. No church contained anything resembling a cult statue such as Phidias' figure of Zeus. The flat pictures in a church did not fill and dominate the interior space as a cult statue did. Every church contained a striking picture of the Son in His human form, but the Father was never represented. No one had ever seen God, but he who had seen Christ had seen the Father. St. Paul, addressing the people of Athens, who were accustomed to the worship of the temples, with their statues, had stated very simply this aspect of the difference represented by the temple and the church:

> The God who created the world and everything in it, and who is Lord of heaven and earth, does not live in shrines made by men. It is not because he lacks anything that he accepts service at men's hands, for he is himself the universal giver of life and breath and all else. He created every race of men from one stock, to inhabit the whole earth's surface. He fixed the epochs of their history and the limits of their territory. They were to seek God, and, it might be, touch and find him; though indeed he is not far from each one of us, for in him we live and move, in him we exist; as some of your own poets have said, "We are also his offspring." [Here Paul quoted the words in which the classical poets Cleanthes and Aratus had characterized Zeus; the phrase very likely had become proverbial]. As

God's offspring, then, we ought not to suppose that the deity is like an image in gold or silver or stone, shaped by human craftsmanship and design.

The Christian God, then, was all that Zeus was and infinitely more; and God's churches were infinitely more than Zeus's temples.

Text and symbolism alike had brought the Eucharist to be the universal recognition and proclamation of the God who has been preached by St. Paul. In this ritual, building and liturgy were closely associated.

To the observer, the Christian ritual might seem to have many affinities with the ancient pagan ceremonies. Processions of clergy and acolytes carrying offerings, candles lighted in the daylight, incense burned in portable censers carried by the priests, music of highly trained choirs—all had their counterparts in pagan worship, where public display had played an important part. Indeed, the Christian worship was in some respects even more elaborate than the pagan ceremonial. The Divine Liturgy, in its fully developed form, required more than two hours and sometimes lasted three, for on occasion there was more than one sermon.

But this high development of the rite was not the ostentation that it might outwardly seem to be. The Liturgy, gorgeous as it was, was not intended as a show or public spectacle. The richness of the setting was, quite simply, considered appropriate—indeed necessary—for the occasion, for what could be more solemn and majestic than the worship of the creator of all things and all men? The act of communion was the most awesome moment in the life of the Christian, and the background had to be suitable for the presence of God accompanied by His angels, as the words of the Cherubic Hymn sang.

The long, stately text of the Liturgy, developed through many generations of Christians seeking to embody their faith and worship in fitting form, was interwoven throughout with texts of the Scriptures. Appropriate psalms were sung at several points in the service, and each day there was a suitable reading from a Gospel and an Epistle. Throughout the service there were hymns, prayers, and litanies, with recitation of the Creed. Some prayers recited by the priest were brief, with responses by the deacon and the choir; others were more elaborate. The whole text of the Liturgy was in fact a study of all the varied aspects of prayer—penitence, intercession, thanksgiving, adoration. The needs of all the community of the faithful, both spiritual and mundane, were remembered. From prisoners and travelers to the imperial family, all Christians were held in mind, including those who had departed from this world. This vision of the Christian community was summed up in one of the closing prayers of the Liturgy:

O Lord, who blessest those that bless thee and sanctifiest those that put their trust in thee, save thy people and bless thine inheritance; protect the whole body of thy Church, and sanctify those who love the beauty of thy house. Do thou endow them with thy divine power and forsake not us who have set our hope in thee. Grant peace to thy world, to thy churches, to the priesthood, to our rulers, to the army and to all thy people. For every good gift and every perfect gift is from above, and cometh down from thee, the Father of lights; and to thee we ascribe glory and thanks and worship, to the Father and to the Son and to the Holy Ghost, now and forever and from all ages to all ages.

The prayers were not only concerned with the community, they were made a means for the contemplation of the nature of God. Many generations of Christians had meditated on the mystery of the divine nature, and it was a part of the purpose of the Liturgy to keep before the minds of the faithful the manifold aspects of this mystery. Just before the communion of the faithful a prayer recited by the priest set forth what man had come to understand of the nature of God and of His sovereign rule:

It is meet and right to praise thee, to glorify thee, to bless thee, to give thanks to thee, to worship thee, in all places of thy dominion, for thou art God ineffable, incomprehensible, invisible, inconceivable, existing always as thou dost exist, thou and thine only-begotten Son and thy Holy Spirit. Thou hast brought us from nothingness into being, and when we fell away didst raise us up again, and thou ceasest not until thou hast done everything, to bring us to Heaven, and confer upon us thy Kingdom to come. For all these things we give thanks to thee and to thine only-begotten Son and to thy Holy Spirit, for all the things we know and do not know, for the seen and the unseen benefits which we enjoy. We render thanks to thee also for this service which thou dost deign to receive at our hands, though thou art surrounded by thousands of archangels and tens of thousands of angels, by the cherubim and seraphim that are six-winged, full of eyes and soaring aloft on their wings . . . .

It was with these thoughts that the people came to the communion. Here the priest prayed to Christ to bestow the gift of His Body and Blood:

Hearken, O Lord Jesus Christ our God, from thy holy dwelling-place and from the throne of glory of thy Kingdom and come and sanctify us, thou who sittest above with the Father and art here invisibly present with us, and do thou deign by thy mighty power to give us of thy sacred Body and of thy precious Blood, and through us to all the people.

After the priest and the deacon had partaken of the bread and wine, the priest rehearsed the story of the Last Supper, and as he administered the consecrated elements to the people, he repeated the words of Christ:

Take, eat; this is my body, which is broken for you for the remission of sins.
Drink, all ye, of this; this is my blood of the new covenant, which is shed for you and for many for the remission of sins.

The hymns that followed summed up the sense of the Presence that came upon the worshipers and their praise and thanks for the mighty act of Christ in the distribution of his Body and Blood, which the faithful could feel sustaining them and all others who had undergone this renewal:

> We have seen the true light, we have received the heavenly Spirit, we have found the true faith, we worship the undivided Trinity: for the same hath saved us.

. . .

> Let our mouth be filled with thy praise, O Lord, that we may sing of thy glory, for that thou hast counted us worthy to partake of thy holy, divine, immortal and life-giving mysteries: preserve thou us in thy holiness, that we may learn of thy righteousness all the day long. Alleluia, Alleluia, Alleluia.

After further prayers and hymns, the Liturgy was at last concluded.

Throughout the whole of the elaborate and unhurried service there were certain themes that constantly recurred, as the eucharistic act, representing the experience of generations of Christians, contemplated the Three Persons of the Trinity and sought to commemorate, in fitting form, both the being and the work of Father, Son, and Holy Spirit. Creation, incarnation, redemption, and glory were brought before the worshiper in a rehearsal of the divine history. But woven in with all this was another idea which helped place the whole history in its true setting.

To every worshiper, the words of the Liturgy had been familiar since childhood, and its ideas had become part of his mind. He could have become so accustomed to the recurrence of the word "all" that the word would seem merely one of the familiar aspects of the prayers and hymns of the Eucharist. Yet, simply and unobtrusively, "all" summed up something that was an essential mark of the orthodox faith, the constant reminder of universality.

The Christian's worship was not merely the Liturgy, celebrated, say, in the Church of St. Sergius at Gaza on the Festival of the Ascension in the third year of the reign of the Emperor Justinian. The prayers and hymns made it infinitely more than that. It was a continuing and a universal act offered "for the peace of the *whole* world . . . and for the union of *all*." "for *all* the clergy and people," "for this city and for *every* city and land." The Doxology, recurring regularly throughout the service, declared that to God "belong *all* glory, honor and worship . . . from *all* ages to *all* ages." God was "a great king over *all* the earth," "worshiped by *all* the host of heaven, who brought *all* things out of nothingness into being," "maker of heaven and earth and of *all* things visible and invisible," "who by Thy boundless power hast formed *all* things, and by the fulness of Thy mercy hast brought forth *all* things out of nothingness into being." Worshiping Him "*all* the days of their life," the congregation prayed "for *all* our fathers and brethren that have fallen asleep before us" and "for *all* pious and orthodox Christians who dwell and are to be found in this city." Mindful of "*all* the saints," the people received the benediction, pronounced by the priest: "The mercies of almighty God and of our savior Jesus Christ shall be with you *all*."

And so the church building, while it was the necessary setting for the act of worship and communion, was never a physical enclosure of the worship and communion. It was a link rather than a location, a link at once vertical and horizontal, joining the members of the Body of Christ in historical time and in present geographical space. The stewards of the mysteries could know that their stewardship was at once an immediate and present ministry and concern and a boundless fellowship. But they could be stewards of their trust only by steady participation in the mystical act of communion, for they knew that they lived surrounded by a mystery and that it was this mystery which was the reality.

Epilogue: The Threads and the Thread

"I never see you going outside the city walls," says Phaedrus. "You must excuse me, dear friend," Socrates replies. "But I am a lover of learning, and fields and trees won't teach me anything; people in the city do."

—PLATO, *Phaedrus*

ONE HUNDRED YEARS after the time of our visit, Gaza, along with Antioch and Alexandria, was swallowed up by the Moslem expansion. Constantinople alone could be leader in carrying on the heritage of the cities.

But if the city of Gaza was detached from the Christian Byzantine world, its share in the heritage was not lost. The city's contribution, once realized, had within it its own life and its own power to survive. The heritage lived not in the material body of the city but in men, and here it could not be obliterated. As Gregory of Nyssa had written, "the storehouses of our memory cannot be destroyed."

Gaza, like other cities, had served as a storehouse of memory and out of this store had helped form the tradition that shaped the spirit of Byzantium and gave the people of the Empire of Constantinople the intellectual and spiritual resources, the national pride and the national hope, which enabled that empire to maintain itself for another eight hundred years and then in due time to transmit its tradition to the West in the day of the Renaissance. The Empire of Constantinople, a vast geographical community with various roots, political, social, intellectual, above all religious, could not have come into being unless it had been able to draw upon the constituent communities, the cities in which people had worked out what they held to be the best activities of human life. It was always in the city that the man of that era thought of finding his full development and fulfillment. The classical city had in its beginning been developed in order to protect and nurture human personality. The city's culture and its whole achievement became embodied in the memory of its people and its teachers. And in his search for his true activity, for his fulfillment, man was held together by his memory.

Thus in the life of Gaza, as it found its culmination in the early years of the sixth century, a new thread was formed of old threads which joined to make something new, at the same time preserving their own particular gifts.

The threads were Judaism, Greek philosophy, Christianity. Moses and Plato, and finally Christ the Word of God, each brought something to men. Israel, Greece, and Rome, and then the new Jerusalem, had come together to create the new empire which made possible the transition from the classical world to Byzantium.

In the case of Gaza, all this had been worked out in the physical setting of an eastern Mediterranean commercial city. The gentlemen of Gaza could not see into the future, and they were perhaps not as conscious of an historic role as our modern study might seem to make them. For them, it was an axiom that the Empire was eternal, just as the Church was eternal.

And so, as we take leave of Gaza, it is in its everyday life that we may once more think of it. As our farewell to the city, we may read the words of the Latin pilgrim to the Holy Land who passed through Gaza in the year 570:

> *Gaza autem est civitas splendidissima et deliciosa, et homines in ea honestissimi, omni liberalitate decori, amatores peregrinorum.*

> Gaza is a splendid city, full of pleasant things; the men in it are most honest, distinguished by every liberality, and warm friends of visitors.

Selected Bibliography

Bury, J. B. *History of the Later Roman Empire from the Death of Theodosius I to the Death of Justinian (A.D. 395–565)*. 2 vols. London, 1923; New York, 1958.

Downey, G. *Constantinople in the Age of Justinian*. Norman, 1960.

———. *Antioch in the Age of Theodosius the Great*. Norman, 1962.

———. "The Christian Schools of Palestine: A Chapter in Literary History," *Harvard Library Bulletin,* Vol. XII (1958), 297–319.

———. "Justinian's View of Christianity and the Greek Classics," *Anglican Theological Review,* Vol. XL (1958), 13–22.

———. "Julian and Justinian and the Unity of Faith and Culture," *Church History,* Vol. XXVIII (1959), 339–49.

Fox, A. *Plato and the Christians*. London, 1957.

Jaeger, W. *Early Christianity and Greek Paideia*. Cambridge, Massachusetts, 1961.

Jones, A. H. M. *The Greek City from Alexander to Justinian*. Oxford, 1940.

————. "Were Ancient Heresies National or Social Movements in Disguise?" *Journal of Theological Studies*, New Series, Vol. X (1959), 280–98.

Mark the Deacon. *Life of Porphyry, Bishop of Gaza*. Translated, with introduction and notes, by G. F. Hill. Oxford, 1913.

————. *Vie de Porphyre, évêque de Gaza*. Edited and translated by H. Grégoire and M.-A. Kugener. Paris, 1930.

Marrou, H. I. *A History of Education in Antiquity*. Translated by George Lamb. New York, 1956.

Meyer, M. A. *A History of the City of Gaza*. New York, 1907.

Mumford, L. *The City in History*. New York, 1961.

Oakley, A. *The Orthodox Liturgy*. London, 1958.

Stein, E. *Histoire du Bas-Empire*. 2 vols. Paris, 1949–59.

Woodward, E. L. *Christianity and Nationalism in the Later Roman Empire*. London, 1916.

Index

165

THE CENTERS OF CIVILIZATION SERIES, of which this volume is the eighth, is intended to include accounts of the great cities of the world during particular periods of their flowering, from ancient times to the present. The following list is complete as of the date of publication of this volume:

4. Roger Le Tourneau. *Fez in the Age of the Marinides.* Translated from the French by Besse Alberta Clement.

5. Henry Thompson Rowell. *Rome in the Augustan Age.*

6. Glanville Downey. *Antioch in the Age of Theodosius the Great.*

7. Richard M. Kain. *Dublin in the Age of William Butler Yeats and James Joyce.*

8. Glanville Downey. *Gaza in the Early Sixth Century.*

UNIVERSITY OF OKLAHOMA PRESS
NORMAN

University of Oklahoma Press

Norman

DATE DUE

15/7/76			
GAYLORD			PRINTED IN U.S.A.